DATE DUE

GAYLORD   PRINTED IN U.S.A.

Programs in Aid of the Poor

Programs in Aid of the Poor

Sar A. Levitan

Fifth Edition

The Johns Hopkins University Press
Baltimore and London

This study was prepared under a grant
from the Ford Foundation.

The Johns Hopkins University Press,
701 West 40th Street,
Baltimore, Maryland 21211
The Johns Hopkins Press Ltd, London

The paper in this book is acid-free and meets the
guidelines for permanence and durability of the
Committee on Production Guidelines for Book
Longevity of the Council on Library Resources.

Library of Congress Cataloging in Publication Data
Levitan, Sar A.
  Programs in aid of the poor.

  Rev. ed. of: Programs in aid of the poor for the 1980s.
4th ed. c1980.
  Includes bibliographies.
  1. Public welfare—United States.   2. Economic assistance,
Domestic—United States.   I. Levitan, Sar A. Programs in aid
of the poor for the 1980s.   II. Title.
HV95.L54 1985   362.5'8'0973   84-28890
ISBN 0-8018-2749-3 (alk. paper)
ISBN 0-8018-2760-4 (pbk. : alk. paper)

Contents

Preface to the Fifth Edition

Nearly two decades have elapsed since the initial publication of *Programs in Aid of the Poor* in 1965. The succeeding three revisions reflected the continued vast expansion of the American welfare system. The second edition recorded the radical changes brought about in the American welfare system by the Great Society. Contrary to the popular image, the first Nixon administration continued to expand the earlier efforts in aid of the poor. As the nation entered its third century, other pressing matters slowed the expansion of the welfare system. New initiatives were halted under the Ford and Carter administrations, although significant progress continued on several fronts. The current Reagan administration represents the most dramatic departure from federal efforts in aid of the poor in half a century. Congressional reluctance to follow the radical retrenchments proposed by the Reagan administration resulted in the retention of most of the federal antipoverty efforts, although at a reduced level. The present edition presents, therefore, an updating of developments and operations of old efforts on behalf of the poor, even if some of their titles have been changed.

The purpose of this study is to review and appraise existing programs in aid of the poor and to explore feasible approaches to the alleviation of poverty in the future. After examining the characteristics of the poor, the study summarizes the major antipoverty measures now in effect, focusing on the operation of the federal welfare system. The system is divided into four separate but related categories: income maintenance programs aimed largely at aiding the poor who are outside the work force; programs supplying goods and services; programs whose immediate goal is to avert the spread of poverty to new generations; and programs to aid the working poor. The final chapter is devoted to a discussion of programs that might be adopted over years immediately ahead.

A *caveat emptor* is in order. This study used various estimates of federal funds allocated to the poor. At present, there is no single agency that maintains such numbers, and even programs targeted to help the poor tend to aid nonpoor people also. The estimates presented in this volume were culled from diverse sources and are intended to indicate rough magnitudes of outlays and trends over time rather than data based on rigorous and hard information.

The reader seeking source materials is invited to turn to the suggested readings at the end of each chapter. The excessive references to my other studies are not because they are the "best," but because *Programs in Aid of the Poor* is based on these studies and they offer the inquiring reader convenient sources for the materials used in the present volume.

I am indebted to Peggy Kelly for her assistance in updating this volume and to Clifford Johnson for his editorial contributions. Without their help there would not have been a fifth edition of the book.

The study was revised under an ongoing grant from the Ford Foundation to the Center for Social Policy Studies of the George Washington University. In accordance with the foundation's practice, complete responsibility for the preparation of the volume was left to the author.

Sar A. Levitan
Center for Social Policy Studies
The George Washington University

Programs in Aid of the Poor

1. The Poor: Dimensions and Programs

If all the afflictions of the world were assembled on one side of the scale and poverty on the other, poverty would outweigh them all.
                                                —Rabba, Mishpatim 31:14

"The poor shall never cease out of the land," according to the Bible. Rather than a pessimistic forecast, this prophecy is an acknowledgment that each society defines poverty in its own terms. It is primarily because poverty is a relative concept that more than one person in seven in this rich country can be designated as poor. In less affluent countries, poverty is equated with living at the brink of subsistence. In this country, even the lowest-income families are rarely confronted with the specter of starvation, though many are the victims of an inadequate diet.

As a relative concept, poverty will always be with us because inequality is a problem in all societies at all times. No system distributes money evenly, nor necessarily should it. The reasons for this inequality of income are many. Some are worthy and some are unconscionable, but the trends are remarkably constant. Income distribution in the United States today is little different from the pattern just after World War II. The poorest 20 percent of all families receive less than one-third the money of the top 5 percent, and there is some evidence that these figures may actually understate the full extent of inequality.

Measuring Poverty

Insofar as it can be measured, poverty can be defined as a lack of goods and services needed for an "adequate" standard of living. Because standards of adequacy vary with both the society's general level of well-being and public attitudes toward deprivation, there is no universally accepted definition of individual or family basic needs. The amount of money income necessary to provide for any agreed-upon set of basic needs is equally difficult to determine. For example, government programs such as free education, subsidized food, or medical care reduce the amount of cash required to support a family. Differentials in the cost of living between urban and

1

rural areas or among regions raise the income requirements for some people and lower them for others. It is no wonder, then, that experts differ over the purchasing power necessary for an individual or family to achieve a minimum acceptable level of economic welfare.

Despite these conceptual and technical problems of measurement, the federal government has devised a poverty index that has gained wide acceptance. Developed by the Social Security Administration in 1964, this index is based on the cost of a minimum diet as calculated by the Department of Agriculture on the basis of a 1955 survey that established an Economy Food Plan for a four-member family with two school-age children (about $2.32 per person per day in 1984 prices). Because families of three or more persons were found to spend one-third of their income on food, the poverty level for these families is set at three times the cost of the economy food plan. This factor is higher for smaller families and persons living alone to compensate for their relatively larger fixed expenses.

Each year the thresholds are adjusted to reflect changes in the level of consumer prices. The poverty thresholds are weighted according to family size, with a larger family having a proportionally higher poverty threshold, and to the age of the householder, with an elderly head presumed to need ten percent less than those under 65 years of age. The federal government's thresholds at the poverty level, based on 1983 prices, are:

Size of family unit	Poverty threshold
One person (unrelated individual)	$5,061
Two persons	$6,483
Three persons	$7,938
Four persons	$10,178
Five persons	$12,049
Six persons	$13,630
Seven persons	$15,500
Eight persons	$17,170
Nine persons or more	$20,310

This poverty index, although offering a constant yardstick against which we can measure society's progress, is imprecise at best. In applying a single standard to all households, varied only according to family size, the index makes no allowance for regional variations in the cost of living. It ignores the predominance of higher prices in central cities, where many of the poor are concentrated, and it also has not been modified to account for the added resources available to those living on farms. The complexity of adjusting the poverty index to reflect regional price differences has impeded further refinements. It remains important to recognize that our official statistics provide only a rough guide to income inadequacy across the nation.

The reliance on cash income in poverty calculations, without regard to its source, also contributes to errors in the official data. By focusing solely on a family's gross income, the poverty index fails to account for differences in tax burdens and other expenses that affect the amount of disposable income available to meet basic needs. For example, a family of four with earnings of $10,180 in 1983 is classified as nonpoor, even though federal income and payroll taxes reduce the household's disposable income to $9,100, well below the official poverty threshold. In contrast, a family of four receiving the same $9,100 in disposable income through tax-exempt transfer payments such as AFDC, social security, and disability benefits is counted as poor in government poverty statistics. The exclusion of family assets in official poverty calculations further weakens the link between a family's poverty status and its ability to secure an adequate standard of living, as households with limited incomes may rely upon savings or property to fulfill basic needs. For these reasons, the distinction between the poor and near-poor is a loose and imperfect one.

A more serious conceptual shortcoming of the current poverty index lies in its failure to include in-kind benefits and assets in determining the size of the poverty rolls. Although nearly three-fifths of all federal aid to the poor is provided through in-kind benefits such as food stamps, health care, and subsidized housing, this assistance is not counted as family income in official poverty data. The reliance solely on cash income has a substantial impact on the number of Americans counted as poor. Officially, they constituted 15.2 percent of the population in 1983. If both cash and in-kind income were counted, however, the 1983 poverty rate could be anywhere from one percentage point lower (14.0 percent) to as much as one-third lower (10.2 percent) than the official rate, depending on the method used for calculating the value of in-kind benefits. Recognizing the importance of in-kind benefits, the U.S. Census Bureau has now begun to supplement the official poverty data with in-kind poverty estimates that include the value of noncash benefits.

Finally, because the official poverty index is necessarily subjective, its adequacy can always be called into question. Critics frequently refer to the original calculation of the official standard in arguing that the present poverty threshold is too low. First, they note that the food costs on which the poverty line is based were developed for "temporary or emergency use" and do not reflect the costs of an adequate, permanent diet. Second, because Americans now spend only one-fourth of their income on food, as opposed to the one-third spent by average consumers in the 1950s, critics argue that the minimum food budget should be multiplied by 4 rather than 3, thereby yielding a poverty threshold considerably higher than the official one.

Others question the adequacy of the official standard because it provides an absolute or static, rather than a relative, measure of poverty in America. The major shortcoming of a static measure— one that adjusts only for changing price levels and not for productivity gains or rising living standards among the general population—is that it fails to reflect changes in aspirations and relative concepts of poverty. As but one example of how our concept of poverty changes, a home without indoor plumbing—the norm in earlier generations—is now considered substandard or unfit for habitation. Yet such shifts in societal norms and expectations, driven by real income gains achieved through greater productivity, are not captured by a static poverty measure adjusted only for changes in the cost of living over time. As a result, the gap between the official poverty level and the nation's median family income has grown in recent decades. In 1960, the median family income was 190 percent of the official poverty threshold for a family of four; by 1983, it had increased to 240 percent of the poverty standard.

A flexible or relative poverty index pegged to median family income would reflect productivity gains as well as changes in the cost of living. For example, if the poverty threshold were set at 50 percent of the median family income, the poverty line for a family of four would be one-fifth higher than the current official level. If adopted, such a relative poverty measure would fail to reflect progress in reducing poverty because there has been little redistribution of income since the 1950s. Low-income Americans have shared in the fruits of economic growth, but they have not won an appreciably larger share of the national income over the past two decades.

The static and relative poverty indexes actually address two distinctly different concerns. A static measure like the official index reveals how the fortunes of low-income households have changed and demonstrates that we have indeed made substantial progress in lifting families above a fixed (albeit somewhat arbitrary) minimum income standard. A relative poverty measure gauges shifts in income distribution, offering a reminder that we have made little progress in sharing the benefits of a prosperous economy more broadly or equitably. The widely accepted official poverty standard will no doubt remain the basis for the government's data collection, and its static measure will provide an important sense of continuity in assessing how low-income Americans are faring. However, for those who view wide disparities in income as a source of concern, relative poverty measures would offer an important supplement to official measures of our progress in aiding the poor.

Our understanding of the level and causes of poverty also can be enhanced through the use of measures that link poverty and employment data and thus provide a more comprehensive picture of labor market conditions and problems. The official poverty index alone fails to reveal whether the poor suffer deprivation as a result of low wages, lack of job opportunities, or nonparticipation in the labor force. A "hardship" measure could shed light on these important questions, yielding valuable information on levels of employment and earnings among the poor as well as on the extent of deprivation among the unemployed and underemployed. Beginning in 1981, the Bureau of Labor Statistics has taken halting steps to provide relevant income and labor market data through the publication of annual reports linking employment problems to economic status. Further efforts to develop a combined index measuring both employment and earnings inadequacy would add significantly to our knowledge of the poverty problem and serve as a valuable guide to federal social welfare policies. In 1984 the Census Bureau initiated the publication of a new statistical series, the Survey of Income and Program Participation (SIPP), which in time will provide data for linking economic hardship with labor force status.

Identifying the Poor

Measured by official government statistics, poverty declined markedly in the decade of the 1960s. In 1960 nearly 40 million persons, or 22 percent of the population, were classified as poor based on the official poverty index. By 1969, this number had been reduced to approximately 24 million, or 12 percent of the population. Most of this progress occurred during the second half of the decade, when jobs were plentiful and the federal government mounted special efforts to extend the gains of an expanding economy to the ranks of the poor.

During the 1970s, however, no apparent headway against poverty was made, and since 1978 the number of poor has climbed steadily. Between 1978 and 1983, 10.8 million Americans were added to the poverty rolls—an increase of 44 percent—as the poverty rate rose from 11.4 percent to 15.2 percent of the population (figure 1). This sharp rise can be attributed to consecutive recessions in 1980 and 1981–82 and to the failure of public assistance benefits to keep pace with double-digit inflation rates during the 1979–81 period.

Without government assistance, the poverty situation would be far bleaker. Almost 25 percent of all families and 37 percent of all unrelated individuals would live in poverty in the absence of cash benefits, a sharp contrast to respective post-transfer poverty rates

Figure 1. Poverty, 1960–1983

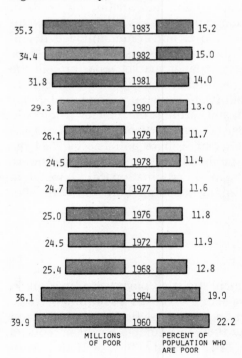

	MILLIONS OF POOR		PERCENT OF POPULATION WHO ARE POOR
1983	35.3		15.2
1982	34.4		15.0
1981	31.8		14.0
1980	29.3		13.0
1979	26.1		11.7
1978	24.5		11.4
1977	24.7		11.6
1976	25.0		11.8
1972	24.5		11.9
1968	25.4		12.8
1964	36.1		19.0
1960	39.9		22.2

Source: U.S. Bureau of the Census

of 15 and 23 percent. If the market value of in-kind assistance were also included, the poverty rate for the 1970s would decline further to approximately 8 percent of the population, followed by a more moderate increase in the 1980s to 10.2 percent. The impact of federal aid to the poor is evident; nonetheless, the nation's increasing affluence makes the deprivation of those who remain poor both more noticeable and more poignant.

The incidence of poverty is related to age, race, sex of family head, work status, and educational attainment (table 1). Blacks are three times as likely as whites to be poor. Families headed by women are four and a half times as likely to be poor as families headed by males. The greatest concentration of poverty is among individuals in female-headed families. Although members of this group constitute only 15 percent of the U.S. population, they account for nearly half of the poverty population. Finally, when the head of the family has eight years of schooling or less, the incidence of poverty is nearly five times that for families headed by a person with some college education. In this sense, the burdens of deprivation fall far more heavily on some groups within the population than on others.

Yet the relative stability of the numbers and characteristics of the poor mask considerable movement of persons into and out of poverty (figure 2). A longitudinal study of 5,000 families by the University of Michigan Survey Research Center found that over a ten-year period, during which time the poverty rate averaged 12 percent, one-quarter of the sample joined the ranks of the poor for at least one of the years studied. This finding suggests that a large segment of the American population is susceptible to at least temporary deprivation, and that poverty is more pervasive than it appears when looking at annual poverty rates. Yet for most households, poverty is not a long-term affliction. Of the families in the Michigan survey exposed to poverty, a majority were poor for only one or two years during the period. Only 2.6 percent of the total sample remained poor for more than seven of the ten years studied. Whites and male-headed families tend to constitute a higher proportion of the transitory poor, whereas only a small segment of the population remains poor and heavily dependent on welfare for long periods of time. Members of this latter group, often referred to as the "underclass," most frequently are poorly educated, aged, black, female, or reside in an inner city. Afflicted with serious behavioral problems, they become trapped in a cycle of poverty and welfare dependency that poses one of the most troubling and complex problems in social welfare policy.

Table 1. Characteristics of the poor, 1983

Characteristics	Persons in families Number (thousands)	Persons in families Poor as % of total in category	Unrelated individuals Number (thousands)	Unrelated individuals Poor as % of total in category
Total	28,434	14.1	6,832	23.4
Age Group				
Under 18	13,705	22.1	102	94.1
18 to 64	13,302	10.8	4,457	21.7
65 and over	1,427	8.1	2,273	26.5
Race of family householder				
White	5,223	9.7	5,291	20.9
Black	2,162	32.4	1,334	40.8
Other races	256	18.4	207	33.4
Spanish origin[1]	933	26.1	370	34.0
Family status				
Householder	7,641	12.3	(X)	(X)
Related children	13,326	21.7	(X)	(X)
Others	6,837	8.8	(X)	(X)
Type of residence				
Central city	10,216	19.0	2,656	23.6
Outside central city	6,983	8.5	1,895	18.6
Nonmetropolitan	11,235	17.0	2,281	29.1
Type of family				
Female householder, no husband present	3,557	36.0	4,213	26.2
All other	4,084	7.8	2,619	19.9
Work experience of family householder				
Full-year, full-time	1,289	3.8	367	3.3
Part-time/part-year	2,476	19.3	3,243	35.4
Did not work	3,845	27.0	4,143	39.0
Armed forces	31	4.5	—	—
Education of family house- holder, age 25 or over				
8 years or less	1,908	22.6	NA	NA
1–3 years high school	1,538	20.5	NA	NA
4 years high school	2,229	10.5	NA	NA
College, 1 year or more	1,003	4.7	NA	NA

Source: U.S. Bureau of the Census.
[1]Persons of Spanish origin may be of any race.
—Represents or rounds to zero.
NA—Not available.

Figure 2. Movement into and out of poverty

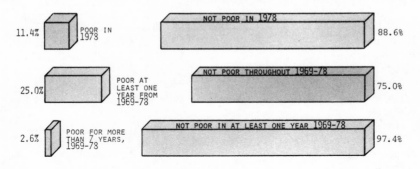

Source: University of Michigan Survey Research Center

A Profile of Americans in Poverty

The demographic characteristics of the poor changed significantly during the past generation. Two phenomena are particularly striking: the increased number of persons living in female-headed households and the decreased number of elderly poor (table 2).

For the purpose of this survey, the poor can be divided into four major groups: the elderly; working-age adults who are employed; those of working age who are not employed; and children, particularly those in families headed by women. Although these groups share the symptoms of low income, their problems vary, and different programs are often required to lift them out of poverty.

The Aged Poor

Traditionally, the elderly have been among poverty's most frequent victims. Throughout the last decade, however, the prospects of older Americans have improved. At the same time that the aged population increased, the number of aged poor dropped from 4.7 million in 1970 to 3.7 million in 1983. This steady decline in the number of elderly poor has left the incidence of poverty among those aged 65 and over slightly lower than that for persons under age 65. Credit for this downward trend in poverty levels for the aged is due largely to more generous social security benefits, which are indexed for inflation, and the growth of private and veterans' pensions.

These poverty figures for the elderly may overstate their gains somewhat because the official data exclude many elderly persons living in publicly assisted housing, as well as others whose own

Table 2. Demographic characteristics of the poverty population over the last generation (numbers in millions)

	1959	1966	1970	1975	1980	1983
Number poor	39.5	28.5	25.4	25.9	29.3	35.3
Percent poor	22.4	14.7	12.6	12.3	13.0	15.2
Aged						
Number poor	5.5	5.1	4.7	3.3	3.9	3.7
Percent poor	35.2	28.5	24.5	15.3	15.7	14.1
Children						
Number poor	17.2	12.1	10.2	10.9	11.1	13.3
Percent poor	26.9	17.4	14.9	16.8	17.9	21.7
Nonaged adults						
Number poor	16.8	11.3	10.5	11.7	14.3	18.2
Percent poor	17.4	10.6	9.2	9.4	10.3	12.6
Individuals in female-headed families						
Number poor	10.4	10.3	11.2	12.3	14.6	16.8
Percent poor	50.2	41.0	38.2	34.6	33.8	35.7
Blacks						
Number poor	9.9	8.9	7.5	7.5	8.6	9.9
Percent poor	55.1	41.8	33.5	31.3	32.5	35.7
Whites						
Number poor	28.5	19.3	17.5	17.8	19.7	24.0
Percent poor	18.1	11.3	9.9	9.7	10.2	12.1

Source: The Bureau of the Census.

income would have classified them among the poor but who live in nonpoor families. It is also uncertain whether progress against poverty among the aged will continue in future years as the economic strains of sustaining a growing elderly population increase. Pressures on both public and private retirement programs, already indicated by raising the eligibility age, removing some of the tax exemption, and cutting benefits to keep the social security system solvent, may well enhance the difficulty of meeting the income needs of the aged in the decades ahead.

The major cause of poverty among the elderly is that few hold jobs. While some of the elderly poor are willing and able to work regularly, the vast majority cannot do so. Their infirmities are doubly critical because an increasing number of elderly persons live alone and must provide for their own support. The best and frequently the only way to help the aged poor is through income support. Provision is also made for high medical costs, which can be devastating for anyone living close to or below the poverty line.

The Working Poor

Lack of employment is often the cause of poverty, but employment itself does not guarantee an adequate income. Close to half of the 7.6 million family heads who were poor in 1983 worked. Many single poor persons under 65 years of age were employed at least part-time. Some combination of low wages, intermittent unemployment, and large families kept these persons and their families in poverty despite their work effort.

Although the link between joblessness and poverty is often overstated, unemployment remains a major cause of poverty. Poor family heads (both male and female) are about four times more likely to be unemployed as nonpoor family heads. In addition, the majority of the working poor who do not experience unemployment encounter other labor market difficulties. Some leave the work force because of illness or disability, and others become discouraged by low-paying jobs and drop out of the labor force voluntarily.

The working poor are heavily concentrated in a few low-paying occupations. For example, although fewer than one-sixth of all family heads who worked in 1983 were employed primarily as private household or other service workers, laborers, or farmers, these occupations accounted for 45 percent of the working poor family heads. At least one family head in five employed in such jobs lived in poverty.

One-half of poor family heads and almost two-fifths of single poor persons worked during 1983 but were unable to climb out of poverty. About one-fifth of all poor families, in fact, had two or more persons working at some time during the year but remained poor. The number of family heads who worked full-time year-round but remained poor declined steadily during the 1960s, and at a faster rate than the decrease in the total poverty population. Nevertheless, by 1983 there remained 1.3 million family heads with about 4.5 million dependents, along with another 367,000 unrelated individuals, who were continuously employed full-time but were still unable to work their way out of poverty.

Employment and training programs designed to smooth the operation of the labor market, enhance the productivity of low-income workers, and open opportunities for employment and advancement can alleviate the plight of the working poor. The acquisition of job skills and work experience are often essential for workers seeking access to higher-paying jobs. Effective enforcement of protective legislation to eliminate discrimination is also required in conjunction with employment and training programs to ensure that opportunities for advancement and self-sufficiency are not closed on the basis of race, sex, or national origin.

The Nonworking Poor

Despite canards about the link between laziness and poverty, most of the unemployed working-age poor are simply not employable—either because of personal handicaps, child care responsibilities, or lack of suitable job opportunities. Illness and family responsibilities are the primary barriers to employment among the nonworking poor. More than one-third of poor males and almost one in six poor females aged 22 to 59 who did not work at all during 1983 were ill or disabled. For male family heads, the percentage was probably higher. In addition, more than three out of every five females in this age group cited home responsibilities as the obstacle to outside work. The problems facing female household heads are particularly acute because the presence of children not only increases income needs and the likelihood of poverty, but also hinders the employment of mothers and therefore reduces (or limits) the income available to meet family needs.

Some of the nonworking poor could and should be lured or goaded into employment. Indeed, a minority are already enrolled in school or training programs that will presumably enhance their employability, or otherwise have searched unsuccessfully for work. With appropriate assistance, work effort and earnings by this group could be enhanced and prospects for self-sufficiency increased. But for the vast majority of these poor, jobs alone are not the answer, and in the absence of some income support their chances of escaping deprivation are low.

Children in Poverty

In 1983 one of every three persons (35.4 percent) classified as poor was a child under sixteen years of age, and nearly one in every four children in the United States lived in poverty. Poverty among children is of special social concern because those raised in poor families are almost inevitably denied opportunities from the very start and are thus impeded in preparing themselves for productive adult lives.

Many children live in poverty because they are its cause—that is, low-income families are frequently driven into poverty by the addition of family members. There is a close relationship between family size and poverty: 56 percent of families with five or more

Figure 3. Poverty and family size, 1983

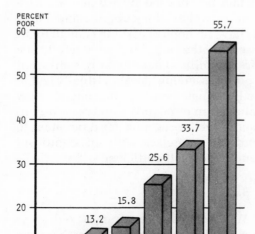

Source: U.S. Bureau of the Census

children live in poverty (figure 3). A higher incidence of poverty among larger families is not surprising in a society where need is ignored as a factor in wage determination, and where the necessity of child care often hinders the wife or female family head from earning needed income.

Poor children have special needs over and above those that can be fulfilled through family income maintenance. Preventive health care, adequate child nutrition, compensatory education, and vocational training are particularly important in providing permanent exits from poverty.

The Feminization of Poverty

Increases in the number of single-parent, female-headed households during the past two decades have clearly made combating poverty in the United States more difficult. Roughly half of all poor families are now headed by women, and female-headed families with children are nearly five times more likely to be poor than other households. Impoverished families headed by women are as a group heavily dependent upon welfare for support, and many female heads of households have no hope of earning enough to lift their families out of poverty even if they are able to obtain full-time work. The rise of single-parent families is particularly significant as an obstacle to economic progress among blacks. Virtually half of black households are headed by single women with generally low earnings capacity. The feminization of poverty deserves a prominent place on the nation's social welfare agenda, for it threatens to create a permanent, dependent underclass with no significant hope of economic advancement and self-sufficiency.

Strategies for Helping the Poor

Poor people need money. Whether they are young or old, their major immediate problem is the lack of income to purchase the most basic goods and services. Beyond this, however, the various groups of the poor have different needs, many of which cannot be filled with liberalized income-support programs. Family heads and young people with their life's work ahead of them must have not only mere daily subsistence but also encouragement and support for acquiring the skills sought by employers. For the aged, medical and nursing home care are primary concerns. Children also need health care and basic education to assure them opportunities in the future. For all poor people, direct provision of housing, medical care, food, and other goods and services serves as an important supplement to income maintenance.

Since the time of the New Deal, the United States has developed a comprehensive, though far from universal, series of programs to assist the economically disadvantaged. This system is based on the assumption that special-purpose programs are required to take care of the diverse needs of the poor. Though some programs single out one or more segments of the poverty population for special attention, other programs overlap in their coverage. Therefore, aid to the poor is more appropriately classified according to the kind of assistance received than by the particular groups that are served.

Federal programs in aid of the poor fall into four broad categories: (1) cash support; (2) direct provision of necessities such as food, shelter, and medical care; (3) preventive and compensatory efforts for children and youth; and (4) employment-related programs and policies designed to expand opportunities for work, advancement, and self-sufficiency.

Income maintenance programs provide the foundation for federal assistance to the poor. Because poverty is generally defined as the lack of adequate income, it can be alleviated most directly by cash support. To the extent that the family unit itself is the best or most appropriate judge of how its limited resources should be allocated, income maintenance also is a more acceptable form of assistance than the provisions of goods and services.

The income assistance approach is not without its inherent problems, however. The probability that need-based payments to employable persons will diminish their incentive to work cannot be ignored. In addition, income subsidies might not be used for the intended purpose of providing basic sustenance. Finally, political support for income maintenance can fluctuate greatly, with semantics playing a significant role. The public may agree to pay allowances to poor people as they undergo training and yet be unwilling to support general relief for the unemployed.

Cash income maintenance programs presently include old age, survivors, and disability insurance (OASDI), unemployment insurance, public assistance, veterans' pensions, and workers' compensation. Because public sentiment against income payments to employable persons apparently remains strong, these programs are aimed for the most part at persons outside the work force or those who have been forced out of jobs. However, more comprehensive programs—such as a guaranteed income, negative income tax, or family allowance—have been proposed to distribute income subsidies solely on the basis of need without regard to labor force status.

Another group of programs provides goods and services directly to the needy as a supplement to their cash income. Whatever the relative merits of helping the poor with cash versus in-kind benefits, political realities frequently dictate the latter. Public attention usually must be focused on a specific and visible problem in order to mobilize society's resources. For example, increased food appropriations were forthcoming only after a highly publicized investigation in the late 1960s stressing hunger in the United States, and the resulting program was tailored to address this specific problem. The food stamp program was expanded further in the mid-1970s as a response to high unemployment. It would have been infinitely more difficult to gain additional support for direct cash payment to the poor, cash that may or may not have been used to purchase a more adequate diet.

Not only is in-kind aid more palatable politically, but some argue that the government is a better judge of needs and priorities than the individual. Moreover, in some instances direct provision of goods is necessary because they are simply not available in the market. For example, in the absence of policies to stimulate construction of low-cost rental units, housing subsidies to the poor would tend to raise rent levels on existing units while doing little to increase the supply of affordable housing, particularly for victims of discrimination. Finally, owing to the economies of large-scale enterprise, the government can in some cases provide a wide variety of goods and services more efficiently than the private sector.

Other services are provided directly by the government not so much to make life easier for today's poor as to give their children a better chance of avoiding poverty. Helping families to have no more children than they want is one of the most effective ways of eliminating poverty. Proper health care and nutrition for mother and child are particularly important to ensure that the young will have better chances for a productive life. The federal government also supports compensatory education programs from preschool through college, allowing children of the poor to develop the basic competencies that are often prerequisites for future opportunities.

The array of federal programs in aid of the poor is completed by employment-related efforts to expand work opportunities and improve the functioning of labor market institutions. These initiatives are designed primarily to eliminate the immediate causes of poverty rather than merely to mitigate its symptoms. For the most part, programs are directed toward the employable poor and concentrate on economic institutions, although increasing recognition has been given to the fact that control over noneconomic institutions can influence access to economic opportunity.

Employment-related initiatives can be divided into three groups: first, programs that seek to improve the individual's ability to compete in the labor market through training, placement, rehabilitation, and incentives to private employers to hire the disadvantaged; second, programs that attempt to restructure the labor market through minimum wage, public employment, and antidiscrimination efforts; third, programs designed to help redevelop depressed urban and rural areas—including Indian reservations—in order to bring employment opportunities to geographic "pockets of poverty."

In the end, of course, these various programs complement and reinforce each other. Not only is it necessary to assuage poverty through cash and in-kind aid, but we should also attempt to prevent tomorrow's by better preparing the young to fulfill their potential and by giving the poor a better chance in the job market. It is not always easy to isolate the impact of government programs upon beneficiaries. Birth control and maternal care may be designed primarily to give the young a better start in life, but they also leave the mother in better condition to contribute to her own support. Similarly, the differentiation between cash support and "rehabilitative" programs is often blurred in reality, as in the case of stipends paid to allow the poor to participate in job training efforts. These interrelationships both caution against narrow evaluations of program benefits and offer a reminder that no single strategy or approach by itself can hope to address adequately the complex poverty problem.

Poverty as a Public Concern

In the modern era, a government role in helping the poor is widely accepted. Yet the notion of government responsibility for the poverty problem is relatively new, emerging in full force only under the strains of the Great Depression. Prior to the 1930s, assistance to the poor was largely left to private charities and religious organizations, supplemented only by public poorhouses and other harsh government institutions. Poverty was perceived primarily as an individual concern and a local responsibility.

The emphasis on private alms and community assistance to the poor was a natural outgrowth of the dominant Western view of poverty. With its origins in Calvinist doctrine and its embodiment in the seventeenth-century English poor laws, this view held that poverty was a product of individual characteristics and failings. For centuries, poverty was viewed as the just consequence of personal inadequacies: physical frailty, mental deficiencies, moral and behavioral defects. Although alms were considered appropriate to relieve the suffering of the sick or disabled, the destitution of the corrupt or weak in spirit was perceived as retribution for their misdeeds. Rooted in this notion of individual responsibility, aid to the poor has for centuries emphasized sharp distinctions between the deserving poor and the deviant, and required moral judgments by neighbors and community leaders at the local level.

Although the widespread unemployment and economic hardship of the Great Depression destroyed public faith in a rigid link between individual characteristics and income adequacy, government efforts to help the poor have continued to be shaped by traditional beliefs. Income maintenance programs still categorize the poor according to labor force status in an attempt to distinguish between the deserving and the deviant, and many federal programs to aid the poor continue to rely upon state or local discretion and administration. Government roles and responsibilities have shifted gradually over time, but the imprint of historical responses to the plight of the poor remains clear.

Prevailing societal values have often dictated that federal assistance to the poor be based on the labor force status of recipients. Even though many poor people move in and out of the work force in response to changing economic conditions or personal circumstances, government programs aimed at the working poor have been distinguished from those designed to help people outside the labor force. Restrictive eligibility and work requirements for those deemed employable, benefit reductions to offset earnings, and low benefit levels for the nonworking poor all are designed to prevent or discourage the "undeserving," able-bodied poor from relying upon government assistance. Ironically, by forcing an all-or-nothing choice between uncertain earnings and the security of a public stipend, these same restrictions have made welfare more attractive than work for many low-skilled, low-wage workers and have added to the financial burden borne by the taxpayer.

With a growing system of income transfers, the decision to work or remain outside the labor force can be complex. Even on theoretical grounds, however, it is difficult to decide a priori which individuals should be provided basic income through work (wages) and which should be provided support through public assistance. For example, should a female head of family with minor dependents and no regular income be required to work for support or should the state assume the obligation of making direct contributions to her family's sustenance? Experts disagree over whether society would be better served by providing work for the mother— assuming jobs are available—or by providing sufficient income to allow the mother to devote her time to raising her children. As the number of working women with young children increases, the latter alternative becomes harder to defend. Yet providing adequate employment for needy low-skilled family heads, particularly when provisions for child care are necessary, can also be a costly proposition.

Throughout the 1970s, the idea that society would be best served by encouraging relief recipients to work without losing all of their welfare benefits seemed to gain increasing acceptance. Provisions for combining work and welfare recognized that low-wage employment by itself often is not sufficient to raise larger families out of poverty, and that incentives for continued work effort offer at least some hope for an eventual escape from dependency. In the early 1980s, the Reagan administration rejected this view, returning to sharp distinctions between the "truly needy" who cannot work and the "undeserving" poor who are presumably employable and capable of self-support. Financial incentives for welfare recipients to work were sharply reduced and in some cases eliminated, and assistance to the working poor with some earnings was cut dramatically under the rationale of targeting benefits to those most in need. The impact of this policy reversal on work effort among the poor is not yet clear, but the Reagan policies undoubtedly have forced low-income Americans to make no-win choices between employment and dependency and have contributed to the travails of the working poor.

During the past two decades, the nation's approach to administration of antipoverty efforts has also come full circle. Prior to the Great Society, most government assistance to the poor was provided at state and local levels; federal social programs were few in number and their budgets correspondingly slim. The federal government provided matching funds for some purposes, including public assistance and vocational education, but administration of these programs was largely left to the states. Even when virtually all financial support came from Washington, as in the case of employment services, the federal role in program design and administration was limited and the traditional bias favoring local community efforts remained.

One of the tenets of Lyndon Johnson's Great Society was that federal expertise and resources could be used to strengthen new government programs and emerging strategies in the war on poverty. The many initiatives of the late 1960s frequently specified national approaches and priorities, providing direct funding to public and private local sponsors without the involvement of elected state and local officials. Narrowly specified grant-in-aid programs proliferated, and funds flowed from a variety of federal spigots. By targeting federal assistance to undeserved groups and conditioning financial support on the fulfillment of numerous program requirements, the enhanced federal role spurred action on problems long ignored by state and local officials. At the same time, however, the expansion of federal categorical programs also resulted in an uncoordinated tangle of services, funding arrangements, and operating guidelines.

By the early 1970s, a reaction against the presumed unwieldiness of the grant-in-aid apparatus had gathered considerable steam. Congress responded in 1972 by enacting the first general revenue sharing program, distributing about $6 billion a year to state and local governments and granting broad discretion in the use of federal funds. Yet the Congress did not abdicate its responsibility for overseeing the design and administration of numerous social welfare programs. For example, in overhauling the many categorical employment and training efforts spawned by the Great Society, Congress rejected in 1973 the Nixon administration's proposed revenue-sharing approach in favor of a federal-state-local partnership. A belief in the importance of federal programs to address unmet national needs, as well as questions regarding the ability and willingness of state and local officials to administer programs for the poor and disadvantaged, caused federal policymakers to retain categorical programs that precluded genuine state or local control.

The Reagan administration, under the banner of New Federalism, gave fresh impetus to the drive for decentralization and decategorization of federal social programs. "Decentralization" generally refers to a decline in the federal role in administering programs, and a concomitant increase in state and local authority. "Decategorization" refers to a reduction in the earmarking of funds for special purposes by Congress, in order to give states and localities broader choice of spending priorities. The administration championed both these goals by reasserting the traditional principle of subsidiarity, which holds that the federal government should not undertake functions that can be performed by a lower level of government. In the realm of social welfare policy, the Reagan philosophy claimed that state and local officials, by virtue of their proximity to those in need, are better able to design and administer solutions to problems in their own states and communities.

The Reagan administration succeeded in advancing these goals through 1981 legislation, increasing state and local discretion in the use of federal social welfare funds by replacing dozens of categorical programs with six block grants in the areas of education, training, health, and social services. It also attempted to shift responsibility for certain welfare programs back to state and local governments, but this initiative failed in large part because of state and local reluctance to accept the additional financial burdens. Despite administration opposition, many other categorical programs have been preserved, allocating federal funds for very specific purposes under narrow and detailed guidelines.

Differing views of the appropriate balance between federal, state, and local responsibility for aid to the poor will always remain. Concerns for equitable financing and state or local inaction will continue to fuel calls for federal initiatives, and demands for manageable administration and responsiveness to community needs will ensure some measure of flexibility and discretion for state and local officials. The American federal system derives its strength from this balance of competing claims and abilities—the danger lies in ideological attempts to push the nation to either extreme.

The Scale of Antipoverty Efforts

The cost of programs in aid of the poor is substantial. Although a precise measurement of their aggregate cost is not possible because non-means-tested programs such as social security and medicare serve the nonpoor as well as the poor, federal expenditures to help the poor were estimated to be $83.8 billion in 1984 (table 3). State and local expenditures raise total government outlays by some 25 percent, with private philanthropic efforts contributing possibly an additional $7 billion dollars if the value of volunteer charitable work is included. Thus, a rough estimate of the total price tag of programs in aid of the poor in 1984 can be set in excess of $100 billion.

As noted above, not all of the resources included in the $83.8 billion in estimated federal expenditures for the poor are allocated on the basis of need. Some programs, such as old age, survivors, disability, and health insurance are not customarily considered to be part of welfare costs because the program's eligibility test is based on prior contributions rather than personal need. Nevertheless, such programs do provide needed assistance to the poor, raising some out of poverty and reducing its severity for many others, thereby warranting the inclusion of benefits received by low-income persons in this estimate of antipoverty expenditures.

For fifteen years after the Great Society focused federal efforts on the elimination of poverty in America, increasing resources were devoted to achieving this goal. By 1979 real federal outlays for the poor had risen 275 percent above 1964 levels, with more than two-thirds of this increase occurring during the 1970s. In the 1980s, however, this trend has been reversed. While total outlays in aid of the poor, adjusted for inflation, remained constant between 1981 and 1984, the young and working-age poor were actually made worse off. Almost all of the increases in current dollar spending during this period went to programs largely benefitting the elderly. Social security expenditures, which are indexed for inflation, rose by $4.4 billion. Outlays for health care, primarily medicare, also increased by $4.4 billion, mainly due to spiraling

Table 3. Estimated federal aid to the poor

Program	1964	1974	1981	1984
	(Billions)			
Total	$7.7	$27.0	$74.5	$83.8
Cash	6.2	11.9	30.9	36.2
OASDI and railroad retirement	3.8	6.3	16.0	20.4
Public assistance	1.3	3.8	9.7	10.3
Veterans' pensions and compensation	0.8	1.0	1.7	1.9
Unemployment benefits	0.3	0.6	1.9	2.1
Earned income tax credits	—	—	0.9	0.8
Other	*	0.2	0.7	0.7
In-Kind	1.5	15.1	43.6	47.6
Employment and training	0.2	2.0	5.9	3.2
Community and economic development	*	0.8	1.1	1.2
Education	0.1	1.8	4.9	5.2
Health	0.7	6.2	15.8	20.2
Housing	0.1	0.8	2.1	2.9
Household energy	—	—	1.2	1.3
Food	0.2	2.4	9.7	10.5
Child care and other social services	0.2	1.1	2.9	3.1

Source: Bureau of the Census, *Statistical Abstract of the United States, 1975* (Washington: Government Printing Office, 1975), p. 405; author's estimates for 1981 and 1984.
*Less than $50 million
—Program not in effect

medical costs which do not improve the standard of living of the poor. Together, social security and health care expenditure increases accounted for almost the entire nominal rise in federal outlays during this period. Consequently, when expenditures for these programs are excluded, real federal outlays for the poor show a 9 percent decline. Considering the increase in the non-aged poverty population from 28.0 million people in 1981 to 31.6 million in 1983 (1984 data not available) the per capita expenditures in 1981 dollars for these non-aged poor indicated an even sharper decline of 18 percent—from $1,771 to $1,450 per poor individual. For the first time since the start of President Johnson's war on poverty, the trend towards increasing federal aid to the non-aged poor has been reversed.

Both as a share of the total federal budget and as a proportion of the disposable income available to all Americans, federal antipoverty expenditures have dropped significantly.

	Percent of total federal outlays	Percent of total disposable income
1964	6.5	1.8
1974	10.1	2.7
1981	11.3	3.6
1984 (est.)	9.8	3.3

It is not possible to render absolute judgments regarding the adequacy of resources allocated by the federal government in aid of the poor. Lacking public consensus on the appropriate level of antipoverty outlays, support for federal expenditures to fight poverty depends ultimately upon perceptions of the severity of deprivation and confidence that government aid can make a difference. The growing gap between the plight of the poor and their deteriorating standard of living in the early 1980s offered, however, ample cause for concern. President Reagan repeatedly undermined public confidence in the ability of government to help the poor. In so doing, his administration both hindered recognition of the nation's prior progress and reversed further improvements in the modern welfare system.

Even though recent political leaders have failed to take credit for its accomplishments, the legacy of the Great Society and its antipoverty initiatives includes major strides toward the elimination of poverty in America that the media have failed to publicize. Poverty as defined by government statistics fell sharply during the late 1960s, and further progress in the 1970s was masked by the failure of official data to take account of expanding in-kind assistance to the poor. A close examination of programs in aid of the poor—ranging from cash and in-kind assistance to services for the working poor and the young—yields evidence of the Great Society's impact and promising prospects for future gains. When the nation rejects the pessimistic notion that government is powerless to help the poor, the lessons of the past two decades will provide a solid foundation from which to launch a more effective and comprehensive assault on poverty in America.

Additional Readings

Burke, Vee. *Cash and Non-cash Benefits for Persons with Limited Income: Eligibility Rules, Recipient and Expenditure Data, FY 1979–81.* Congressional Research Service, Report No. 83-110 EPW, June 1983.
Congressional Research Service, Library of Congress. *How Can the Federal Government Best Decrease Poverty in the United States?* National

Debate Topic for High Schools, 1984–1985. Washington, D.C.: U.S. Government Printing Office, 1984.

U.S. Congress, Subcommittee on Oversight and Subcommittee on Public Assistance and Unemployment Compensation of the Committee on Ways and Means, House of Representatives. *Background Material on Poverty.* Washington, D.C.: U.S. Government Printing Office, October, 1983.

U.S. Bureau of the Census. *Annual Statistical Abstract of the United States.* Washington, D.C.: U.S. Government Printing Office, 1983.

U.S. Bureau of the Census. *Money Income and Poverty Status of Families and Persons in the United States.* Current Population Reports, Series P-60, annual volumes. Washington, D.C.: U.S. Government Printing Office.

U.S. Bureau of the Census. *Population Profile of the United States.* Current Population Reports, Series P-23, annual volumes. Washington, D.C.: U.S. Government Printing Office.

U.S. Congressional Budget Office. *Major Legislative Changes in Human Resources Programs Since January 1981.* Washington, D.C.: U.S. Government Printing Office, August 1983.

Discussion Questions

1. Who are the poor in the United States and why are they poor?
2. How accurate are the Current Population Survey poverty estimates? What are the major shortcomings of these measurements?
3. Given the increase in employment and welfare outlays during the 1970s, why has there been no reduction in the number of poor persons during the decade? Why has poverty increased between 1978 and 1983?
4. Compare the pros and cons of counting the number of poor based on an arbitrary income level as contrasted with a poverty threshold based on a predetermined proportion of median individual or family income.
5. Do you believe that poverty would disappear within the next generation if 3 percent annual average growth in productivity is resumed?
6. "Inequality of family income is an inevitable characteristic of our economy." Discuss.
7. "This Federal Government of ours, by trying to do too much, has undercut the ability of individual people, of communities, churches, and businesses to meet the real needs of society as Americans always have met them in the past." Evaluate this statement by President Reagan.

2. Cash Support Programs

You shall open wide your hand to your brother, to the needy,
and to the poor.   —Deuteronomy, 15:11

Nearly three of every ten Americans received assistance from public programs in 1984. The total cost of the programs was $418 billion, three-fifths of which were cash payments. The poor are much more likely to receive cash transfer payments than are the nonpoor (figure 4), although many of the nonpoor would have been poor without these transfers. An estimated 23.1 million persons were kept out of poverty in 1982 by cash transfers.

Social Security Act

The Social Security Act, the product of five decades of evolution since its enactment in 1935, is by far the most significant income maintenance program for both the poor and the nonpoor. Programs contained in this act accounted for 91 percent of the cash support received by Americans in 1984, and for about 88 percent of cash payments to the nonpoor. Two groups of programs included in the act were: (1) social insurance programs—including old age, survivors, and disability insurance and unemployment insurance, both of which distribute payments on the basis of prior earnings and payroll contributions; and (2) public assistance programs—for the elderly, the blind, the disabled, and families with dependent children—which provide income support on the basis of need alone (figure 5).

OASDI

The social security system is vast. Old age, survivors, and disability insurance expenditures alone totaled $179.2 billion in 1984 (excluding $62 billion paid for hospital and medical insurance). Some 36.2 million persons—one American in six—received regular cash payments. Coverage is extensive: nine of every ten people in paid employment or self-employment are covered; of those who

Figure 4. Sources of income, poor and nonpoor families, 1982

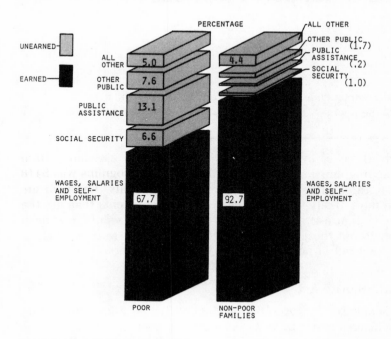

Source: U.S. Bureau of the Census

reached age 65 in 1984, only 6 percent were not eligible for some benefits; 95 percent of all children and their mothers would receive benefits if the father were to die. Old age insurance provides income to a steadily rising portion of the aged population—up to 92 percent in 1980. Only 8 percent of those aged 65 and over are not eligible for benefits.

Individuals must be insured in order to receive benefits. Persons who contribute payroll taxes for a minimum of 40 quarters (10 years) are permanently insured. The basic benefit payable to a retired or permanently disabled worker is related to the worker's age when he or she retired and to the level of covered earnings. (Two exceptions are: a special benefit of $130 per month for persons who reached age 72 before 1968 and who had no covered work, and a minimum benefit of up to $357 for workers with prolonged years of covered employment at low wages.) Dependents and survivors can receive set proportions of this benefit, subject to a family maximum. Social security benefits are not

Figure 5. Government outlays for income security cash payments

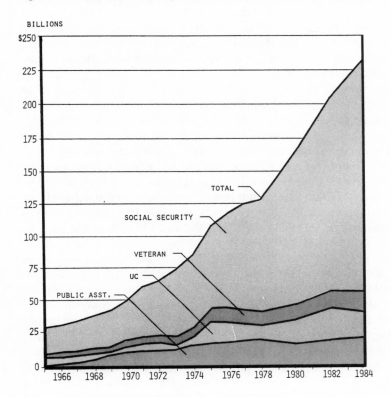

BILLIONS

Source: Budget of the United States Government, Fiscal 1985

means tested, but they are reduced if the recipient continues to work. In 1985, payments for beneficiaries aged 65 to 69 are reduced one dollar for each two dollars earned above $7,320. "Earnings" include income from labor, but not income from rents, royalties, dividends, or pensions.

Survivors insurance is also payable to an insured worker's surviving children under 18 years of age, to the parents of these children (until the children reach age 16), to dependent parents of the deceased worker, and to dependent widows or widowers. Finally, disability insurance aids severely disabled adults (aged 18 to 64) unable to engage in substantial gainful employment. To be eligible for insurance payments, they must have worked in at least 20 of the 40 quarters (five of the ten years) prior to becoming disabled or, in the case of workers disabled before age 31, they must have worked half of the quarters (but not fewer than six) since turning 21. Disability benefits are paid after a five-month waiting period, and medical proof of disability is required, along with a determination that the disability rules out gainful employment. One-fifth of the estimated 13 million work-disabled adults receive disability insurance.

The extent to which OASDI should redistribute income is widely debated, but it now does so in two ways. It replaces a higher percentage of lost income for lower-paid workers than for higher-paid workers. It also transfers money from those now working to those who are retired, disabled, or the survivors of deceased workers. OASDI may be viewed as a kind of compulsory "insurance" in the sense that it operates on the principle of risk-pooling and pays benefits without an individual test of need; however, it differs from commercial insurance by not keeping reserves in hand adequate to meet all claims. Under recent legislation, OASDI is planned to operate as a partially funded system.

Despite several recent increases, benefits remain inadequate to raise all recipients above the poverty threshold. In 1984 about 6 percent of cash beneficiaries aged 65 and over also received means-tested welfare supplemental security payments. The average monthly benefit of $443 in August 1984 left the retired worker just barely escaping poverty, but the average retired couple received benefits 20 percent above the poverty level (figure 6). An individual with the minimum benefit would receive $229 per month, almost half the poverty level. To protect the income of retired workers from inflation, the law provides that benefits be adjusted when the cost of living rises by 3 percent or more annually.

OASDI distributes more income to the poor than any other government transfer program. One poor family in five receives these benefits. These income supports have prevented many households from falling into poverty. However, because eligibility and benefit levels are based on past earnings rather than current income, social security is not the most cost-effective approach for aiding the poor, even among the aged.

Until the 1970s, both the benefits and the burden of funding OASDI fell disproportionately on the bottom of the income spectrum. Since low-paid workers and those with large families were not exempt from payroll contributions, but upper-income wage earners paid payroll taxes on only a portion of their earnings, the flat-rate tax constituted a relatively heavier burden on those households. On the other hand, lower-income workers benefit disproportionately, receiving a much higher percentage of their average indexed monthly earnings (AIME) once they retired. For example,

Figure 6. Social Security benefits, August 1984

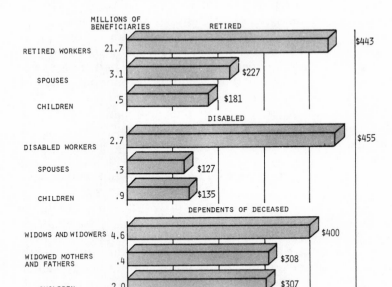

Source: U.S. Department of Health and Human Services

a beneficiary who worked all of his or her life at the minimum wage for an AIME of $262 would receive a benefit level equal to 90 percent of this amount, or $236. Retirees with higher monthly earnings receive an additional 32 percent of any average earnings above $267 but not exceeding $1,612, so that a worker whose AIME was $800 would receive a monthly benefit of $411 (90 percent of $267 plus 32 percent of $533). Retirees in the highest income brackets receive benefits equal to only 15 percent of their average indexed monthly earnings above $1,612. As a result, an individual with an AIME of $2,000 would receive a benefit of $665 per month, almost one-third of total average earnings.

In the face of growing concern for the solvency of the social security system in the early 1980s, the relative burden of the payroll tax on upper-income Americans has been increased substantially, thereby minimizing its traditionally regressive impact. As part of the 1977–1983 social security amendments, Congress has repeatedly raised the ceiling on the amount of earnings subject to payroll taxes so that the cap now covers the total earnings of most workers. In 1985, the social security system will be financed by a 14.1 percent tax (including 2.7 percent for health insurance) on annual earnings up to $39,600, shared equally by employer and employee. Since the employer's contributions are part of the worker's defined earnings, the total tax amounts to about one dollar of every seven of the employee's compensation.

The 1983 social security amendments also made a portion of benefits paid to higher-income beneficiaries subject to federal income tax. As of January 1984, up to one-half of social security benefits may be taxed for single taxpayers with incomes exceeding $25,000 or married taxpayers who file jointly with incomes over $32,000.

Financial pressures on the social security trust funds prompted Congress to raise the retirement age from 65 to 67 by the year 2027. At present, workers receive their full entitlement upon retirement at age 65, but approximately 70 percent of retiring workers with social security benefits choose early retirement for one reason or another. To discourage drains on social security funds, those retiring at age 62 have their benefits reduced by 20 percent, and this reduction is scheduled to increase to 25 percent by the year 2009 and 30 percent by 2027. On the other hand, workers can increase their benefits by 3 percent for each year beyond 65 (up to age 72) they postpone retirement, and this increment will gradually rise to 8 percent by 2008. The rewards for work by beneficiaries will also increase in 1990, after which payments will be reduced by only one-third of earned income instead of the current one-half.

The 1983 bipartisan compromise on social security financing included difficult changes in both payroll taxes and benefit structures. Its adoption is expected to prevent further fiscal crises in the social security system at least during the 1980s. However, some of these reforms clearly work to the detriment of the poor. For example, because many of those who choose lower benefits are actually forced into earlier retirement by job loss or disability, and because they typically have lower average earnings than workers who wait until age 65, a permanent reduction in the benefits of early retirees seems harsh.

Public Assistance

In addition to distributing benefits under OASDI to insured workers or their survivors, the Social Security Act provides Aid to

Families with Dependent Children (AFDC) and assistance to the aged, blind, and disabled through the Supplemental Security Income (SSI) program. Persons not eligible under one of these federally aided programs may receive state-funded and locally funded general assistance. AFDC accounts for over two-thirds of the 16.3 million recipients and nearly half of the almost $17 billion in 1984 federal expenditures. AFDC is identified with "welfare" because it accounted for most of the increase in means-tested income support after World War II (figure 7).

SSI generally offers substantially higher benefits than AFDC and general assistance. Although public assistance lifts many persons out of poverty, almost 80 percent of those reporting public assistance income in 1982 remained poor even after receiving this aid.

Aid to Families with Dependent Children

AFDC is not only the costliest but also the most controversial public assistance program. In May 1984 there were 10.9 million recipients, including 6.8 million children, or nearly one child in every nine. Benefits paid during fiscal 1984 totaled over $14 billion. The federal government pays an average of 55 percent of AFDC costs, with state and local governments paying the remainder. States with below-average per capita incomes receive a higher federal matching share, in some cases exceeding 70 percent of total AFDC costs. The share that localities contribute to AFDC is determined by individual states, and constitutes less than 5 percent of total costs nationwide.

Although the federal government contributes more than half of the total cost of AFDC, it delegates administration of the program to the states within broad federal guidelines. More important, the federal government has left it to the states to determine eligibility standards and the level of benefits. For purposes of determining eligibility, gross income, after exclusions, is limited to 150 percent of the state's standard of need. The standard nominally reflects the cost of rent, utilities, food, clothing, and other basic expenses. In many states, however, there is little correlation between actual living costs and the established need standards. The monthly cost of basic needs calculated by the states for a family of four on AFDC in July 1983 ranged from $201 in Texas to $911 in Vermont; the median was $470. In two-thirds of the states, the standard of need is set below the poverty threshold, making many families with meager earnings ineligible for benefits.

Many states fail to pay benefits equal to these low standards of need under AFDC. Varying rules determine the difference between

Figure 7. AFDC accounted for most of the public assistance growth in the last three decades

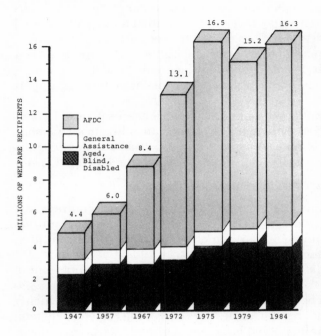

Source: U.S. Department of Health and Human Services

need and public assistance payments. Only twenty-five jurisdictions provide AFDC payments equal to their full standard of need. Others set maximum benefits below the standard, often paying only a fixed percentage of the standard. In fifteen states the maximum amount paid to a family with one adult and three children and no other income is less than two-thirds of their need standard. No state pays high enough benefits to keep an AFDC family out of poverty in the absence of other income or in-kind assistance, and states with relatively low per capita income tend to pay lower benefits. The real value of the median state maximum payment under AFDC declined by 36 percent between 1970 and 1983, so that the average state maximum payment to AFDC families of four was $368 in 1983. Given the stinginess of standard need definitions, the failure to set payments at least equal to this prescribed level leaves most public assistance recipients in deprivation. Map 1 shows the range of average benefit payments and the parsimony of some states.

Map 1. Average monthly AFDC payments per person and family, March 1984 (Family payments in parentheses)

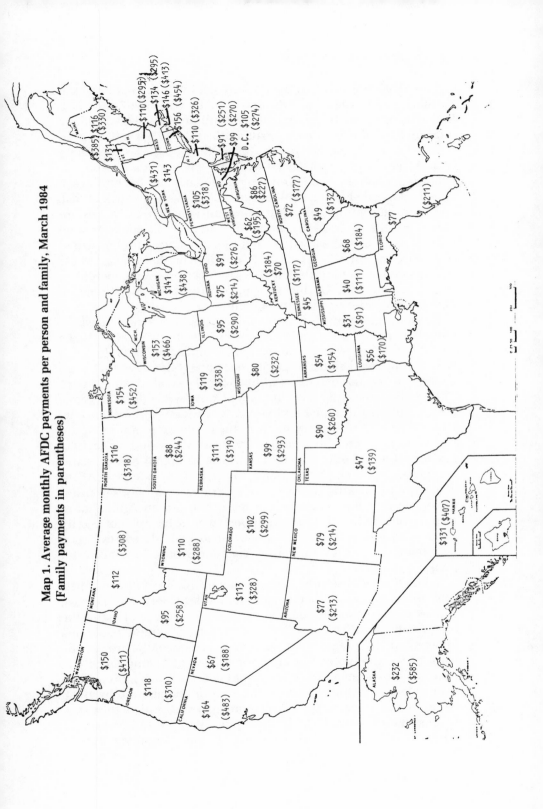

The AFDC rolls grew rapidly after World War II, doubling each decade between 1947 and 1967 and again between 1967 and 1972. Since the early 1970s, this expansion virtually ceased (except for a mild increase during the recession in the mid-1970s and again in 1982). The rapid AFDC growth during the 1960s was especially remarkable because it occurred while the poverty population was declining. Changes in eligibility requirements and benefit levels, growth of female-headed families (including out-of-wedlock births), and more accepting public attitudes all contributed to this increase. By the early 1970s, however, the bulk of female-headed poor families had already qualified for assistance, and the size of the AFDC population stabilized. Finally, in the 1980s, AFDC benefits (adjusted for inflation) were reduced and some recipients forced off the rolls by the Reagan administration's policies of budget cuts and overall retrenchment.

Federal legislation and Supreme Court decisions influenced the growth of the welfare population during the 1960s and early 1970s by extending coverage to groups not previously eligible. In 1961, Congress allowed states to grant assistance to families that were dependent because of the unemployment of an employable parent. This "unemployed parent" component, now available in 21 states, the District of Columbia and Guam, covers only those working fewer than 100 hours per month—those working any more are ineligible no matter how meager their earnings—and since 1981 has been limited only to families whose principal earner is unemployed. In 1968, the Supreme Court further extended AFDC eligibility by striking down so-called "man in the house" rules, under which many states held a man living in an AFDC house responsible for the children's support even if he was not legally liable. The following year, the court also invalidated residency requirements used by numerous states to restrict eligibility for public assistance.

While these developments were increasing the number of persons eligible for assistance, neighborhood legal services agencies, welfare rights organizations, and other groups were publicizing the availability of AFDC benefits and helping potential recipients understand the program's eligibility requirements. Through the work of these advocacy groups, the stigma of "being on relief" declined. Government income support became much more widely distributed, reaching almost one-third of the population by 1984. AFDC recipients alone constitute more than one-tenth of the populations of New York City, Philadelphia, Baltimore, Chicago, St. Louis, Detroit, and the District of Columbia. Improvements in administration further facilitated the expansion of AFDC rolls by shortening delays between application and approval.

Population growth in the quarter century after World War II swelled the ranks of potential AFDC recipients, increasing the number of children in the United States from 42 million in 1945 to more than 69 million in 1972. Of greater importance, however, were changes in family structure that increased the number of households headed by women. The dramatic rise of single-parent, female-headed households during the past two decades has prompted extensive debates regarding its cause. Critics of AFDC and other public assistance contend that these programs induced families to modify their behavior in order to qualify for benefits, encouraging a man to either desert his family or refuse to marry so that his dependents would qualify for assistance. Others stress that the causality is far from clear, and that welfare benefits may simply provide women with the financial ability to choose an independent household over an unsatisfactory marriage.

Regardless of cause and effect, the underlying trends in family formation are clear. Not only did the rate of divorce increase 50 percent during the 1960s, but the number of children involved per divorce decree also increased. Although data are imprecise for desertions and separations without court decree—the "poor man's divorce"—these also grew more frequent. But claims that mothers on welfare have additional children in order to qualify for higher payments are not substantiated by data. In fact, the average AFDC family has 2.9 persons, and six of seven AFDC households have four or fewer persons. There may be some substance, however, to the charge that the availability of AFDC has encouraged out-of-wedlock births; during the 1960s out-of-wedlock births multiplied from one in twenty to one in ten.

Finally, AFDC growth during the 1960s and early 1970s was fueled by the increasing attractiveness of welfare benefits relative to other sources of income. As the federal government assumed a larger share of the burden, states became less reluctant to qualify individuals for aid and to provide more adequate benefits. Between 1947 and 1962, average payments and spendable average weekly earnings of all private employees rose equally; but between 1963 and 1978, AFDC payments increased 162 percent while earnings rose only 130 percent. Significant increases in the use of food stamps and medical payments—not reflected in the cash payments—tilted the balance even more in favor of welfare. (These in-kind income supplements are discussed in chapter 3.) Work still provides the greatest source of income for poor families (see figure

4). Yet growing numbers of families found that they could maximize their income by combining these two sources, and public policies during the 1970s encouraged this mix of work and welfare as the most effective means of reducing deprivation and promoting self-sufficiency.

Some of the factors that contributed to the rapid expansion of AFDC in the 1960s—most notably the rise of female-headed households—persisted in the following decade. But state cutbacks in real benefits, public reaction against more generous welfare provisions, the imposition of new work requirements on recipients, and a decline of 7 million in the number of children between 1972 and 1982 decelerated the growth in AFDC rolls after 1972. The number of AFDC recipients peaked during the 1975 recession at 11.3 million, declined in the latter half of the decade, and rose again following the 1982 recession. Although administration officials attributed this leveling off to better management, others believed that most eligible persons had already joined the AFDC rolls.

President Reagan took office in 1981 with the goals of reducing public assistance costs and discouraging welfare dependency. His administration quickly sought to focus federal aid on the "truly needy," which it defined at those who could not be expected to work and lacked other means of support. It was assumed that strict work requirements and reductions in aid to the working poor could be used to promote self-sufficiency, forcing employable individuals in impoverished households to provide for themselves and their dependents. These principles guided Reagan's proposals for welfare retrenchment, which were incorporated in the Omnibus Budget Reconciliation Act (OBRA) passed by Congress in the summer of 1981.

By rejecting policies of the 1960s and 1970s that used positive financial incentives to encourage low-income people to work, the Reagan reforms fell most heavily upon recipients who combined work with welfare. The administration virtually repealed a 1969 law that allowed reasonable work expenses, the first $30 of earnings, and one-third of additional earnings to be disregarded in computing monthly welfare benefits. Under the new OBRA provisions, the "$30 and ⅓" earned-income disregard was restricted to the first four consecutive months of employment, after which time the work incentive bonus no longer applied. Furthermore, a monthly ceiling of $75 was placed on work-related expense deductions for full-time employment, along with a $50 ceiling on part-time employment and a $160 per child ceiling on child care expense deductions. These provisions have combined to undermine work incentives for those on the welfare rolls and reduce federal aid to the working poor.

The changes sought by the Reagan administration were explicitly designed to remove employable individuals from the AFDC rolls. Approximately 50 percent of the 450,000 to 500,000 AFDC recipients with earnings in 1981 lost their eligibility under the OBRA provisions, costing those households both marginal income support and guaranteed health care coverage under medicaid. Another 40 percent of working AFDC recipients lost some portion of their benefits. Other provisions of OBRA also served to restrict AFDC eligibility, including requirements that part of the income of step-parents be devoted to child support and that the value of family assets not exceed $1000, a significant reduction from the more liberal levels of allowable assets under prior law.

The most explicit attempt by the Reagan administration to discourage reliance upon AFDC benefits was embodied in an OBRA provision authorizing states to operate work relief programs, commonly known as "workfare." Under the workfare program, states can require specific categories of welfare recipients to work without pay at the locally established rate, but not below the minimum wage, for a number of hours sufficient to "earn" their welfare benefit. The concept of making welfare recipients work off their grants was further reinforced in the Tax Equity and Fiscal Responsibility Act of 1982, which permitted states to require job search upon application for benefits. Thus, while the Reagan retrenchments have reduced the financial incentives for AFDC recipients to seek work, the administration also resorted to more forceful means to induce welfare recipients to enter the labor market.

It has been estimated that OBRA changes in AFDC pushed 600,000 individuals below the poverty line in 1982, independent of the effects of that year's recession. Partly in response to this growing poverty population, Congress took steps to soften the impact of the OBRA welfare cuts in 1984. These provisions, which took effect at the start of fiscal 1985, raised qualification levels for AFDC assistance from 150 to 185 percent of a state's standard of need, thereby extending eligibility to a wider range of low-income families. Positive work incentives were also reinstated to induce more people to combine work with welfare. The $30 earned income disregard was extended from 4 months to 12 months, although the 4-month limit on the additional one-third disregard remained. In addition, the monthly work expense deduction of $75 for full-time workers was applied to part-time workers as well.

Finally, the 1984 changes allowed families receiving monthly child support payments to keep the first $50 per month without counting such support as income in determining their AFDC benefits.

Data on the characteristics of AFDC recipients are skimpy. The latest survey by the Department of Health and Human Services contained no information about the education level of half of the recipients or about the labor force experience of another one-quarter. Any insights about AFDC participants are based upon partial data that may not be representative of the total population. Given these reservations about the quality of the data, it would appear that AFDC recipients are disadvantaged in many ways, but they are not a class unto themselves. AFDC families are pre-dominantly female-headed; fathers are present in only one AFDC home in eleven. The majority of AFDC fathers are not in the labor force and in two out of three of these cases they are incapacitated. Forty-three percent of AFDC families are black and fourteen per-cent are Hispanic. AFDC mothers have substantially lower edu-cational attainment than adult women in general: only three out of seven completed high school, compared to five out of seven of the entire adult female population. Their work experience also tends to be severely limited. Nearly one-fourth have never been em-ployed, and of those who have worked, one of three are employed in services, including private household, clerical, or as unskilled laborers, occupations that generally provide meager earnings. The average number of children per family was 2.1, but over one-third of the children had parents who were not married to one another.

Hope of moving a segment of the AFDC population toward work and self-sufficiency remains plausible. The characteristics and aspirations of AFDC recipients have become increasingly similar to those of the American people as a whole during the past two decades. About one-fourth of adult female recipients and over two-fifths of adult male recipients are either working or looking for work, and these proportions are slowly rising. Their educational attainment, although still relatively low, is also rising. More have some paid work experience. Most significantly, studies have shown that AFDC recipients are no less eager to work than the rest of the population.

Just as poverty is often transitory, most families do not languish forever on welfare. Although the employability of many AFDC mothers is limited, it has become more acceptable for a female family head to work and child care facilities are expanding. For example, in 1979 (the most recent year for which such data were compiled) nearly three of every ten AFDC families had received welfare benefits for less than one year, and a majority of families had remained on the rolls for less than four years. Fewer than 8 percent of all AFDC families had received assistance without interruption for more than ten years, thereby approaching a generation of long-term dependency. Research tracking the welfare participation of a representative sample of 5,000 families throughout the 1970s yielded similar findings: although the percentage of the total population receiving public assistance in any given year remained a constant 10 percent between 1969 and 1978, only two percent were dependent on welfare for their primary support for more than eight years of the survey period. For the remainder, a combination of work and welfare was the norm.

Supplemental Security Income

For nearly four decades, assistance programs for the aged, blind, and disabled operated similarly to AFDC. Although the federal government contributed a share of the cost, state and local governments largely determined eligibility and benefit levels and administered the programs. Benefits were more generous than under AFDC, but they too varied widely from state to state.

Social security amendments passed in 1972 thoroughly revamped this system. The federal government now provides a basic monthly benefit for the aged, blind, and disabled under the Supplemental Security Income (SSI) program. As of January 1985, the federal benefit rate was $325 per month for an individual living in his own household with no other countable income, and $488 for a couple. Although the initial federal SSI guarantee passed in 1972 was higher than benefits previously paid by nearly half the states, the guarantee represented about 76 percent of the poverty level for individuals and 84 percent for couples. States can supplement the federal rates if they choose, but without federal contributions.

Under the revised SSI program, federal eligibility standards replaced demeaning eligibility criteria required by many states to ensure that only the most destitute received benefits. A lien on a welfare recipient's property netted little for the state but took a heavy toll in self-respect. However, the federal law did retain other stringent standards. Aside from a home, an automobile with current market value under $4,500, property for self-support, and life insurance policies with a total face value of $1,500 or less, the assets of aged, blind, or disabled public assistance recipients cannot exceed $1,600 for an individual or $2,400 for a couple. The intent of the law is to protect the taxpayer from the claims of those not in need, without debasing the recipient.

The 1972 law also provided that the first $20 per month of social security payments, or other unearned income, plus the first $65 of earned income and half of additional earnings be disregarded in computing SSI eligibility. It is ironic that the law offers the aged, blind, and disabled—whose ability to work is often limited—more attractive incentives to work than recipients of AFDC, many of whom can and should be encouraged to work. One explanation for this difference is that the Congress anticipated a relatively low price tag in approving liberal work incentives for the aged, blind, and disabled, whereas the cost of similar incentives in AFDC would be far higher.

Congress designed these changes in minimum benefits and work incentives to channel more income to the aged, blind, and disabled. Adjusting for inflation, program costs remained relatively stable during the revised law's first decade and amounted to an estimated $9.4 billion in 1984. Much of the numerical increase occurred because SSI benefits, like OASDI benefits, are indexed to price inflation. This is one of the major differences between federally administered SSI and the state-run AFDC programs, which are not automatically increased for inflation. SSI benefits still are not uniform across the nation, because 26 states and the District of Columbia offered additional payments totaling $1.6 billion in 1984. The average monthly number of recipients rose from 3.1 million in fiscal 1972, the year prior to the enactment of SSI, to almost 4 million two years later. The SSI rolls have remained at this level throughout the past decade.

The majority of SSI recipients are old, white, and female:

	Median age	Proportion white	Proportion female
Aged	78	55	74
Blind	55	59	58
Disabled	54	60	60

The number of aged recipients has declined by nearly one-half from its peak in 1950 under the three separate programs, a trend generally attributed to the extension of the social security system. As the number of aged welfare recipients dropped from 2.8 million in 1950 to 2.0 million in mid-1984, the number of OASDI recipients aged 65 and over grew from 2.6 million to 25.6 million. The proportion of SSI recipients who also received OASDI climbed steadily to 70 percent during this period.

The aged were typically alone and without other support. Only one in six lived with a spouse, though close to ten of every eleven maintained their own household. Only 13 percent had unearned income other than social security benefits, which averaged $73 a month. Their capacity for self-support was meager, not at all surprising among a population with an average age of 77 and almost two of every five above age 80. Only 1.3 percent of recipients were working in late 1983. Of the 27 million persons 65 years of age and over in 1982, nearly one in seven, or 3.7 million, were poor. The number of aged poor declined by over one million during the preceding decade largely as a result of higher welfare benefits, including social security, supplementary security income, and veterans' benefits.

The number of blind SSI recipients has also declined since the 1950s. Almost nine of every ten blind persons on SSI lived in their own households. About 8 percent were under 18 years of age. Remarkably, over 6 percent of SSI recipients were working full or part time, but a significant proportion had never worked. Many had one or more chronic health problems in addition to blindness.

Aid to the disabled began only in 1951. In contrast to the declining ranks of aged and blind SSI recipients, the number of disabled recipients increased steadily to the 2.3 million mark by 1984. The disabled are afflicted by a variety of impediments, both mental and physical. Seven of every eight disabled adult recipients maintain their own households. The proportion of disabled recipients who are confined to their homes has dropped significantly in recent years. Only a relatively small proportion of disabled recipients also receive vocational rehabilitation.

The aged, blind, and disabled are less capable of self-support and considered less responsible for their dependency than AFDC recipients; hence, they are deemed more "deserving" of aid. This public judgment is clearly reflected in notably higher benefits and more humane administration under SSI than under AFDC. However, the more generous SSI benefits also reflect the potential impact of a federal guarantee on disparate state provisions for the poor. A federal minimum AFDC benefit, frequently advocated as part of comprehensive welfare reform proposals, could be expected to have a similar effect.

General Assistance

For the needy who do not qualify for federally supported aid, most states provide varying coverage and benefits through general assistance. Some provide cash payments; others limit assistance to medical care, hospitalization, or burial. In 1983 there were almost 1.3 million persons on general assistance rolls in 40 jurisdictions. The monthly outlay per recipient amounted to $127 in 1980, resulting in a total program cost for that year of $1.4 billion. Five states—Illinois, Michigan, New York, Ohio, and Pennsylvania—accounted for 70 percent of the caseload and expenditures. Clearly, most states made very meager provisions for persons who do not qualify for federally supported income programs. In Pennsylvania, there was one general assistance beneficiary for every three AFDC recipients; in California, one for every 25; and in South Carolina, one for every 1,100.

General assistance cases are concentrated in large cities. The total number of recipients has fluctuated considerably over the years, typically rising during economic slumps. Because of rapid turnover, the number of persons receiving general assistance benefits during a year may be twice the number of recipients at any given time.

Veterans' Compensation and Pensions

Income support on a preferential basis has long been available to a select segment of the population—the 28 million veterans and their 60 million dependents and survivors. This type of income support predates even the Revolutionary War. Colonial laws mandated public support for men incapacitated in defense of the community. Although present programs do not provide enough support to permit all veterans and their dependents to escape poverty, they go a long way toward providing basic needs, particularly for older veterans and indigent survivors of deceased veterans.

Two types of cash benefits—compensation and pensions—were provided to veterans at a cost to the federal government of $13.9 billion in 1984 (figure 8). Compensation is paid to veterans (or their dependents) for an injury, disability, or death incurred while serving in the armed forces, and pensions are paid to war veterans (or their dependents) whose annual income is below a specified level and who are permanently and totally disabled. In practice, the disability qualifications for a pension are relaxed as the veteran advances in age. The pension qualifications are more stringent for veterans below the age of 55, but veterans aged 65 and over may qualify on the basis of need. Altogether about one-fifth of total cash payments to veterans go to poor people.

Compensation

One of every thirteen veterans received compensation in 1984 for service-connected disability at a total budgeted cost to the government of over $8 billion. Individual annual compensation averaged

Figure 8. Veterans income support, 1984

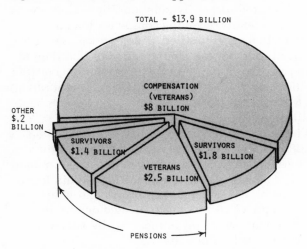

Source: Appendix to Budget of the United States Government, Fiscal 1985

$3,676, ranging from $768 for a 10 percent disability to $15,060 for a total disability. The payment to veterans with 30 percent or more disability is supplemented for dependents. Additional special monthly compensation paid to veterans who suffered total blindness, deafness, or loss of limbs may boost the payment to $42,984 annually.

Congress periodically raises the level of compensation benefits to keep pace with rising living costs. Average annual compensation costs are likely to increase somewhat even in the absence of a rise in benefits because service-connected disabilities tend to become aggravated with advancing age. However, the higher mortality rate of injured persons diminishes the potential rise in benefits if these veterans were to live out their normal life span. Four of every ten World War II veterans who were receiving compensation in 1983 qualified for only minimum disability benefits (10 percent impairment), compared with just one of every five World War I veterans. At the other extreme, almost one of every ten World War I veterans who were receiving compensation were totally disabled, compared with one of every twenty World War II veterans. Because older veterans are more likely to suffer severe impairment, the average monthly compensation for World War I veterans was significantly higher than for World War II veterans—$366 as compared to $280 in 1983.

Data are not available on the current income level of veterans receiving service-connected disability compensation. However, a 1971 study found that veterans receiving compensation had lower annual incomes than their nondisabled peers, and many of the disabled would have been counted among the poor had they not received compensation. This is particularly true of the 506,000 (out of a total of 2.3 million in 1983) whose degree of impairment was 50 percent or more. Many of these disabled veterans were probably unable to hold full-time jobs.

A total of $1.8 billion in survivors' benefits was distributed in 1984 among 345,000 dependents of service persons who died as the result of military service. Survivors' benefits are provided under two separate programs: death compensation is paid to survivors of service persons who died in action prior to January 1, 1957, roughly one-seventh of all service-connected deaths; dependency and indemnity compensation is received by survivors in cases of service-related deaths since that date.

Death compensation pays a flat annual rate of $1,044 to a surviving spouse, $1,841 to a widow or a widower with one dependent child, and $900 to a dependent parent. Rates of dependency and indemnity compensation vary with the rank held by the deceased veteran. Annual stipends range from $5,532 for a recruit's widow to $15,180 for a chief-of-staff's widow. The basic entitlement is increased $53 a month for each dependent child, $68 a month for a widow who is housebound, and $139 a month for a widow who is in need of aid and attendants. Compensation alone barely places widows of low-ranking veterans above the poverty threshold; however, most widows with dependent children and those over 62 years of age are eligible for concurrent social security benefits.

Death compensation is paid without regard to other income received by survivors or dependents. Similarly, dependency and indemnity compensation is not subject to a means test except in the case of qualifying dependent parents. Parents are eligible for support if their income does not exceed $6,273 for a single parent or $8,435 for both parents. Maximum benefits of $3,084 and $4,392, respectively, are reduced in relation to other income.

Pensions

A total of three-quarters of a million war veterans received $2.5 billion in disability pensions in 1984, an annual average of $3,365 per veteran. These pensions are paid under three separate systems. The first two programs apply only to those veterans who qualified for pensions prior to 1978. Under these two protected programs, a veteran would continue to receive the same level of benefits as in 1978, regardless of changes in his income, as long as that income remained below $6,273 in 1984 for a veteran without dependents and $8,435 for a veteran with dependents.

All veterans qualifying for pensions since 1979 are covered under the third system. This new system resulted from a Congressional restructuring of the entire pension system that linked pensions to total family income and provided cost-of-living adjustments concurrent with the increases in social security benefits. The benefit payment is equal to the difference between the veteran's income and the maximum allowable benefit payment of $5,515 for a single veteran and $7,225 for a veteran with dependents. A single veteran with an annual income of $1,000 is entitled to a $4,515 pension, giving a combined income of $5,515. A veteran with $2,000 of annual income would receive a pension of $3,515, giving the same combined income of $5,515 as received by the veteran with only a $1,000 prebenefit income.

Dependents of deceased veterans may qualify for pensions. Benefits are paid to surviving spouses and unmarried children under age 18 (or age 23 if they remain in a VA-approved school) who meet applicable income standards. Provisions are generally made for a veteran's child only when orphaned and receiving no other support from parent or guardian.

Altogether, 870,000 survivors received almost $1.4 billion through veterans' pensions in 1984, with an average benefit of $1,578 per family. Between 1965 and 1980, the number of widows of deceased World War II veterans who were receiving pensions more than tripled. If recent trends continue, the number of widows of World War II veterans qualifying for pensions will rise as the mortality rate of these veterans increases and qualifying income levels are relaxed.

Since most veterans' widows with children also qualify for social security benefits, the combined potential income of veterans' survivors has significantly reduced the number of poor. Almost half of pensioned widows, however, still remain below the poverty threshold.

In contrast to the public assistance programs, veterans' benefits are administered with maximum consideration to the recipients' dignity and self-respect. Provided the veteran can prove eligibility, he or she has only to file a simple form in order to qualify. Thereafter the veteran is required to submit annually only the information needed by the Veterans Administration to keep the claim current and active. The annual data are filed on a simple form supplied to the veteran or the dependent, which includes information about the veteran's assets, income, and dependents eligible to receive benefits.

Once eligibility is established, the Veterans Administration makes only a cursory check on claims. Although the General Accounting Office has criticized these methods of certification, the Veterans Administration insists that the trust is justified, since spot checks made with the Internal Revenue Service in cases of questionable claims show that the incidence of false claims is small. Assistance to veterans and their surviving dependents continues to be delivered with a minimum of delay. The system is worthy of emulation by other public assistance programs in which onerous and costly needs tests are made at the expense of services to the needy and at little savings to the taxpayer.

Unemployment Insurance

The objective of unemployment insurance (UI) is to provide essential aid to workers during periods of forced idleness. Unemployment insurance was not designed as an antipoverty program, but as a protection earned by the worker against joblessness. Eligibility for payments and the level of benefits are based on past earnings and work experience and not on need, so the poor are often excluded or receive meager benefits. The purpose of unemployment insurance is to cover nondeferrable expenditures without reducing the recipient's incentive to work.

Unemployment insurance was established along with the other social insurance programs under the Social Security Act of 1935. However, it was given a unique administrative structure. The law imposed a payroll tax on employers in all states. In 1984, the tax rate was 3.5 percent of the first $7,000 of an employee's annual earnings, with more than three-fourths of the resulting revenues (2.7 percent of applicable earnings) returned to the states for the operation of their own programs. Effective in 1985, the tax rate was raised to 6.2 percent, 87 percent of which (5.4 percent of applicable earnings) is returned to the states. The federal portion of UI tax revenues are earmarked for the administrative costs of the program and the federal-state extended benefit program.

Although state programs are subject to a few federal requirements, including standards that specify covered industries and workers, the states determine the duration and amount of benefits, the eligibility of the covered worker, and the amount of the employer's contribution through a system that reduces the tax burdens of employers who have a low unemployment experience. Not surprisingly, employers encourage state statutes that include as many barriers to qualification as possible. As a result, individual state programs vary widely even though the tax is universal. Three additional unemployment insurance programs are administered by the federal government for veterans, railroad workers, and federal government employees.

In order to establish eligibility for unemployment benefits, a worker forced from covered employment into idleness must meet the state's employment and earning tests, be available for work, and register with the local employment service office. Normally, the unemployed are also required to report weekly on their job search efforts. About 97 percent of all wage and salary workers are covered under the unemployment insurance provisions of the Social Security Act or one of the three separate federal unemployment compensation programs. Many of the excluded workers are state and local government employees and farm and domestic workers. The latter two groups are characterized by low income and intermittent employment, leaving them particularly vulnerable to poverty.

States have additional eligibility rules that may exclude the poor from unemployment compensation. The covered worker typically must have been employed during two of the last five quarters, and many states require that earnings during the qualifying period be at least thirty times the weekly benefit amount or a flat minimum sum ranging from $600 in Nebraska to $1,700 in New Hampshire. These minimum earning requirements force low-wage earners, who are most susceptible to unemployment, to work longer than high-wage earners in order to qualify for unemployment benefits. Also excluded are those unemployed who are just entering or reentering the labor force and those who either have been terminated for misconduct or have quit their jobs voluntarily. These and other criteria disqualify more than half of all unemployed persons at any given time.

A related problem (and one that is more significant to the poor) concerns the relationship of unemployment benefits to those who leave the labor force to enroll in employment and training programs. In many states, the unemployed are ineligible for UI benefits if they are undergoing training because they are not immediately available and looking for work. Further, stipends paid to institutional training enrollees do not count toward UI eligibility, so that enrollees encountering difficulties in locating employment after leaving such a program are not entitled to unemployment benefits.

Weekly unemployment insurance benefit amounts vary widely among states. Most states compute benefits as a fraction of the worker's weekly or quarterly earnings, with maximums that are fixed amounts or fixed proportions of the state's average weekly wage; in thirteen states, allowances are made for dependents. In 1984, maximum benefits for a claimant with dependents ranged from $105 per week in Mississippi and Missouri to $278 in Massachusetts. Minimum benefit levels, on the other hand, are set as low as $5 per week, with the highest weekly minimum being $60 but such a benefit floor still helps very low wage earners.

The duration of benefits is often as crucial to the recipients as the average weekly payment. Until the early 1970s, maximum duration of payments was normally 26 weeks. As a cushion during periods of rising unemployment, Congress in 1970 authorized an additional 13 weeks of benefits in all states when the national seasonally adjusted insured unemployment rate (IUR) exceeded 4.5 percent for three consecutive months. The 1981 Omnibus Budget Reconciliation Act, however, repealed this national trigger. Under this revised legislation, individual states are permitted to extend benefits for a 13-week period when their insured unemployment rate exceeds 6 percent, or is at least 5 percent and is also 20 percent higher than the average IUR for the preceding two years. This change in the law limits the availability of extended benefits for the long-term unemployed, many of whom are poor.

In recent years, Congress has responded to rising joblessness in recession years by granting further temporary extensions of unemployment insurance benefits. Despite the Reagan administration's intent to curtail unemployment benefits, the severe recession of 1982 prompted Congress to authorize an additional 8 to 14 weeks of payments for jobless workers who had exhausted their thirty-nine weeks of eligibility. These extended benefits, financed entirely by federal revenues, were made available until March 1985.

The more comprehensive protection provided to unemployed workers during the recessions of 1975 and 1982 carried a substantial price tag, with total costs reaching $17 billion in fiscal 1976 and soaring to over $29 billion in fiscal 1983. The persistently high levels of unemployment in the early 1980s created serious financial problems for the unemployment insurance fund. The heavy debt incurred by many states forced revisions in the UI program, but these changes had little effect on the poor.

Frequent and prolonged unemployment continues to be a significant cause of poverty. It is likely that an increase in average benefits under unemployment insurance programs and the relaxation of eligibility based on earnings would reduce the number of jobless Americans who slip into poverty, or at least bring them closer to the poverty threshold. The effectiveness of unemployment benefits as an antipoverty device, however, is limited by its structure as an insurance program. During 1982, only an estimated 17 percent of unemployment benefits were paid to the poor. As long as the amount and duration of benefits are dependent on past work experience, those in the lowest paid occupations with the highest incidence of poverty will be helped the least.

Workers' Compensation

Workers' compensation, like unemployment insurance, is designed to protect individuals and families during a period when wages are reduced or interrupted due to work-connected injuries. In addition to cash benefits, the workers' compensation system provides medical care and rehabilitation services for injured workers. Finally, the program compensates workers' survivors in the event of fatal injuries.

Workers' compensation is administered similarly to unemployment insurance in that each state has broad discretion over its own compensation program. In recent years, benefit levels for the disabled have risen substantially. In the majority of states, the maximum weekly benefit for a totally disabled worker is at least equal to 100 percent of the average weekly salary in the state and in 43 states the maximum payment equals or exceeds the cash income ($200 per week) required to raise a four-member family out of poverty. A weakness of the present system is that temporarily disabled persons get about the same benefits as the totally and permanently disabled. Lowering the benefits paid to the temporarily disabled would induce them to resume work as soon as they are able.

Workers' compensation laws cover approximately 87 percent of the labor force. Most farm and domestic workers and other low-earning casual workers, however, are excluded from coverage in many states, and an estimated eight of ten recipients of medical care are not off the job long enough to receive cash payments. In 1982 program expenditures totaled $16.1 billion. Cash benefits accounted for $11.3 billion, and another $4.8 billion was devoted to medical and hospital care. Unfortunately, injured workers requiring medical rehabilitation receive scant attention. When available, vocational services received by the disabled workers are most often the result of efforts by employers and insurance carriers who have a vested interest in restoring the injured workers' productivity.

Private Pensions

Social security benefits alone often leave their elderly recipients near or below the poverty threshold. For a growing proportion of retirees, OASDI is supplemented by benefits from private pension or profit-sharing plans that insure a more adequate standard of living. Though an accurate count of private pensions is not available, it is estimated that more than half of all employees in the private sector and three-fourths of all civilian federal, state, and local government employees are covered by a pension or profit-sharing plan. Eligibility requirements have been liberalized significantly over the last decade, increasing the proportion of covered workers ultimately qualifying for retirement benefits. It is estimated that more than 35 percent of all retired workers received some private retirement benefits by the end of 1982.

The private pension system has important ramifications for poverty among the elderly. Almost all workers covered under private plans are also covered by social security. Through a combination of the two, most recipients are assured of escaping poverty in their "golden years."

Congress enacted a pension reform law (ERISA) in 1974 and strengthened it in subsequent years to safeguard the integrity of private pension funds and to protect the pension rights of employees who change jobs. In 1984, Congress passed ERISA amendments designed to make it easier for women to qualify for pensions and to collect survivors' benefits under private pensions in the event their spouses die before retirement, a significant step to reduce poverty among female retirees. Despite these improvements, however, the impact of the private retirement system on poverty remains limited. Benefits are paid out of funds accumulated through wage deferrals and higher-paid workers are more likely to be covered. The private retirement system is primarily a way for middle- and upper-income families to insure against poverty in old age, rather than a means to protect low-income workers.

Taxing the Poor

Several income tax provisions are intended primarily to diminish the federal tax burden of the poor and can be viewed, in a sense, as indirect income payments. Of particular importance to the poor are the additional tax exemptions for aged and blind persons and the tax exclusion of major government income transfer programs. In fiscal 1985, these measures accounted for an estimated one-eleventh of the total personal income tax revenues foregone by the federal government:

Exclusion of social security benefits	$17.8 billion
Exclusion of unemployment insurance benefits	1.8 billion
Exclusion of public assistance benefits	0.5 billion
Exclusion of veterans' benefits	2.2 billion
Additional exemption for the aged and blind	2.7 billion

Although these amounts are not usually reflected in budget totals, they nonetheless provide substantial benefits to recipients.

During the 1970s, the anomaly of the poor paying income taxes at the same time that society sought to raise their income prompted revisions in the federal income tax structure. Both the standard deduction and personal exemption were periodically raised to ensure that most families in poverty would not pay federal income taxes. The 1985 standard deduction was set at $2,415 for a single person and $3,570 for married couples, and the personal exemption at $1,050. To lighten the tax burden on low-income persons and to offset a portion of federal payroll taxes, Congress approved in 1978 an Earned Income Tax Credit (EITC), which allowed families with dependent children to claim a tax credit equal to 10 percent of their earned income up to $5,000 (for a maximum credit of $500). The amount of the credit decreased for households with higher earnings and reached zero when earned income reached $10,000. In 1985, the EITC rate was increased to 11 percent, allowing a maximum credit of $550 and a partial credit for households with earnings up to $11,000. Because this tax credit is refundable, the EITC works like a negative income tax for impoverished families with low earnings.

The sweeping tax cuts championed by the Reagan administration in 1981 lowered federal income tax burdens for middle- and upper-income Americans, but the minimal benefits provided for the lowest wage earners have been completely offset by federal payroll taxes and inflation. As a result, the number of poor persons who pay federal income taxes has doubled since 1980, and total federal tax burdens for many impoverished families have doubled or tripled since 1978. A family of three living at the poverty line paid only $35 in federal income and payroll taxes in 1978, but its tax burden soared to $546 by 1984. Tax liabilities for a family of four with an income at the poverty threshold rose from $269 in 1978 to $1,076 in 1984, while federal taxes paid by a family of six at the poverty line jumped from $523 to $1,523 during the same period.

Because of the failure of the Reagan administration to preserve the real value of the standard deduction and personal exemption, the principle that poor people should not be forced to bear a sizable federal tax burden has been seriously undermined. In 1984, a family of four with income $1,800 beneath the poverty threshold, as well as a family of six with income $4,000 below the poverty line, paid federal income taxes. Furthermore, the Census Bureau estimated that over 3 million persons with gross incomes above the poverty level had their disposable income pushed below the threshold by federal income and payroll taxes. Total federal and state income and payroll taxes paid by the poor have increased by 60 percent during the first half of the 1980s, making rising tax burdens a serious threat to progress in aiding the poor.

Aside from personal income taxes, other taxes on the poor remain burdensome because of their regressive impact. The social security tax (7.05 percent in 1985) continues to fall most heavily upon low-paid workers, although recent increases in the maximum earnings subject to payroll taxes have reduced this inequity. State and local sales taxes also pose an increasing burden, failing to exempt those on welfare or even the poorest of the poor. Many jurisdictions have sales taxes of 5 percent or more, and some jurisdictions tax food and other necessities. Neither payroll nor sales taxes provide allowances for workers with large families, who have the greatest chance of joining the ranks of the working poor.

Income Maintenance Proposals

Administrative problems, the stinginess of benefits in some states, gaps in coverage, rising costs, and the continued existence of a large number of poor have led to several proposals to supplement or replace existing income maintenance programs with a more comprehensive form of cash assistance. Three basic alternatives which have been proposed by previous administrations are (1) either a guaranteed income or negative income tax, (2) children's allowances, and (3) employment guarantees or wage subsidies. The first two approaches are discussed below; public employment and minimum wage provisions are discussed in chapter 5. Even though the Reagan administration has rejected these proposals, thereby forestalling any current action on them, they are still worthy of mention for future consideration.

Negative Income Tax

The simplest method of eliminating poverty would be to make up the income deficit of the poor in order to guarantee a pre-determined, socially acceptable minimum income. For example, in order to lift its total income to the official poverty threshold ($10,178 in 1984 dollars), a family of four with an income of $6,000 a year would receive a grant of $4,178. If the family had no income, it would receive $10,178. Such a program would require an esti-mated annual outlay of $46 billion.

A central objection to a simple income guarantee is that it would reduce pecuniary work incentives for millions of people, since their incomes would remain at the poverty threshold whether or not they held jobs. To counter the possibility that such workers would decide to forego employment for the dole, any workable plan must allow low-wage earners to keep at least a portion of their earned income. One proposal would exempt half the earnings of low-income families in qualifying for payments. Thus, a family of four with an income of $6,000 would count only $3,000 for nega-tive tax purposes and be able to claim $7,178 for a total income of $13,178, compared with the $10,178 maximum paid to a family without a wage earner. Such provisions would, of course, increase the cost of the program beyond the amount needed simply to bring all poor people up to the poverty threshold. The magnitude of the increase would depend on the level of incentives offered by the plan. However, it is reasonable to suppose that the annual cost of the plan might rise to at least double the amount needed to bring every family's income to the poverty threshold.

The income tax structure offers the most convenient vehicle for administering such income guarantees. Though currently geared only to the collection of taxes, the reporting machinery could be adapted to distribute grants and cover income deficits—a negative income tax.

Advocates claim that the negative income tax would substitute a single, comprehensive program of income maintenance for the existing plethora of efforts. Although its simplicity is appealing, the idea does present several problems. As in the case of the poverty index, the income guarantee could not easily compensate for cost-of-living differentials between urban and rural areas or among various cities and regions. Reliance on personal income tax returns would also necessitate the determination of a family in-come, altering present filing arrangements substantially. Finally, the timing of negative income tax payments would raise numerous issues. Disbursing benefits every April 15th is obviously inadequate. However, monthly benefits based on the prior month's earnings, for example, may not provide timely relief to a family during a particularly lean period; paying on the basis of expected earnings may introduce distortions because of inaccurate estimates. The timing of benefits and recertification of eligibility have presented problems under AFDC and will continue to do so under a negative income tax scheme. Furthermore, some mechanism must be retained to provide assistance in emergencies.

A crucial problem in the proposed system is the selection of a base level of benefits and a "marginal tax rate," or the formula by which assistance is reduced as earnings rise. Benefits must be adequate for those who cannot provide for themselves and incentives must be attractive enough to induce the able-bodied to contribute to their own support. A low tax rate is of no help to those who cannot work, whereas a high benefit level may draw able-bodied workers out of the labor market. The availability of unearned benefits may decrease the earnings differential between skilled and unskilled workers and may dampen the incentive to acquire skills. Combining a high benefit level with a low tax rate could qualify many middle-income families. Ever present as a constraint on benefits and incentives is the cost of such a program. Taxpayer backlash at the high cost of welfare keeps benefits low.

This trade-off among benefits, incentives, and cost is present in any public assistance system. There is no "correct" answer, and choosing the best combination remains a question of personal values.

Family Allowances

Another method of providing cash assistance to the poor is to pay families with children an allowance or income supplement to meet a portion of childrearing costs. This proposal recognizes that the wage system alone distributes income inadequately because wages are based on productivity or tradition rather than on need. While the principle of equal pay for equal work is desirable as a means of eliminating discrimination based on color, age, or sex, it ignores the differing needs of families and tends to deprive children in large families of basic necessities. The underlying justification for family allowances is that a child's well-being should concern society as a whole.

Our wage system takes little or no account of the diverse needs of workers. Except for adjustments in income taxes, for example, the take-home pay for a given job is the same for a bachelor as for the head of a family with dependents. Despite the wide acceptance of family allowances in other countries, the idea has never received active consideration in the United States—although it has been advanced on numerous occasions. AFDC is in a sense a form of family allowance, but expenditures under this program accounted for only about 0.4 percent of national income in 1984. A number of countries spend a greater share of their national income for family allowances.

Family allowances are now paid in all industrial nations except the United States. These allowances vary widely in benefit patterns, adequacy, and financing. In some countries eligibility is universal; in others no benefits are paid for the first or second child. Benefits are usually paid for children up to the age they would normally leave school, but may be extended for further full-time schooling, training, or apprenticeship. The allowance per child also varies widely. For example, Sweden pays a uniform rate for all children, while France has a complex system that adjusts for family income, size, and children's ages.

The adequacy of benefits ranges widely. In Australia, the allowance for two children equals 4.6 percent of the average weekly wage, compared with 20.8 percent in France. For four children, benefits varied from a low of 8.2 percent in Canada to a high of 45.4 percent in France. Just as benefits per child vary from country to country, so does total outlay. As a proportion of the gross national product, expenditures for children's allowances in 1979 ranged from 1 percent or less in Sweden, Australia, and Canada to about 1.3 percent in West Germany, France, and the United Kingdom.

Children's allowance benefits are usually financed by the national government out of general revenues. Many countries reinforce cash outlays with tax deductions for children. Both methods increase a family's resources for rearing children. However, Sweden eliminated the latter when it adopted the former, and the United States has only the latter.

Family allowance programs are not a complete alternative to negative income tax and are certainly no substitute for existing welfare assistance to the aged or to others without children. But because family size is so closely correlated with poverty, family allowances would lift many adults out of poverty along with their children. Universal family allowances have several advantages over other forms of income maintenance. There is no need for an income test, a feature that would reduce administrative costs and maintain work incentives. Because the program distributes benefits to all children, it would probably be more politically acceptable than any alternatives. The major obstacle to family allowances is the belief that, in an era when the dangers of overpopulation are very real, such a program would encourage procreation. This apparently has not been the case in other countries with such programs, and in any event childbearing would not be a profitable enterprise under any of the programs that have any chance of passage. Nonetheless, family allowances could be coupled with effective birth control programs to reduce the potential number of unwanted children.

Alternative Income Support Proposals

Reflecting dissatisfaction with the operations of the welfare system, a number of alternatives for reform have been proposed and debated over the years. Although no action has been taken towards implementing these reform measures during the Reagan administration, they—like the income maintenance proposals—are worthy of mention for future consideration.

From the discussion on welfare reform, a few vital issues have emerged: the level of assistance, incentives and requirements to work, and the overlap with in-kind benefits. The costs to taxpayers embodied in the various proposals are also a crucial consideration in selecting alternatives to aid the poor.

Most of the suggestions cover all families with children, thus adding to AFDC families the "working poor" but not the poor without children. One proposal, however, would add a "demogrant," or payment to each person, regardless of family status. Instead of the fragmented AFDC program, in which each state operated independently but with federal contributions, the federal government would establish a uniform minimum nationwide benefit schedule. Proposed benefit levels range from half of the poverty threshold to 50 percent above it. The lower level of support would constitute an increase over AFDC payments in only a few states. The states, however, would not be prevented from supplementing the federal payments. The maximum proposal would include a broad chunk of the populace and would be extremely expensive. In some versions the payment is solely a transfer, but in other proposals public service jobs would be available at low rates of pay to supplement low base payments.

Determining who is employable and whether employable family members should be encouraged or required to work is another stumbling block. The most lenient proposals include no coercion, allowing welfare mothers to choose whether to stay home with their children or go to work, and offer attractive incentives to work, permitting recipients to keep up to two-thirds of their earnings. Others envision harsh requirements that recipients find employment, take make-work jobs, or undergo training, and include paltry work incentives of as little as one-third of earnings.

Meshing cash assistance with existing in-kind programs presents two thorny problems. First, each program provides that benefits be reduced as earnings increase. These reductions are not coordinated, however, so the cumulative "marginal tax rates" for the several programs sometimes approaches or even exceeds 100 percent. This means that recipients *lose* economic benefits by working more. Second, some variations disqualify recipients of cash relief from obtaining certain in-kind benefits. The increased cash, it is argued, would more than substitute for loss of food stamps. But this is not always true. Not only would some families gain only a few dollars to compensate for the loss of several hundred dollars in in-kind benefits, but other families, in states paying more than the federal minimum, would lose the in-kind aid and receive nothing at all in return.

The rapid growth of food stamps, medicaid, supplemental security income, and unemployment benefits has increased the number of variables to be considered in reform. A debate with so many combatants and so many issues could result in legislation only after considerable political compromise. Of particular significance in the legislative debates is that income support is recognized as a federal responsibility and that a consensus has emerged on the desirability of providing a guaranteed income for at least part of the population. The feasibility of combining work and welfare has gained acceptance from some, but current policies have kept it far from becoming a viable approach to welfare reform.

Additional Readings

Aaron, Henry J. *Why Is Welfare So Hard to Reform?* Washington, D.C.: Brookings Institution, 1973.

Ball, Robert M. *Social Security: Today and Tomorrow.* New York: Columbia University Press, 1978.

Levitan, Sar A.; Rein, Martin; and Marwick, David. *Work and Welfare Go Together.* Baltimore, Md.: Johns Hopkins University Press, 1972.

Salamon, Lester M. *Welfare, the Elusive Consensus.* New York: Free Press, 1980.

U.S. Department of Health, Education and Welfare. *Social Security in America's Future.* Final Report of the National Commission on Social Security. Washington, D.C.: U.S. Government Printing Office, March 1981.

U.S. Department of Health and Human Services. *Social Security Bulletin: Annual Statistical Supplements.* Washington, D.C.: U.S. Government Printing Office.

Veterans Administration. *Annual Report.* Washington, D.C.: U.S. Government Printing Office.

Veterans Administration. *Federal Benefits for Veterans and Dependents.* Washington, D.C.: U.S. Government Printing Office, January 1984.

U.S. Congressional Budget Office. *Welfare Reform: Issues, Objectives, and Approaches.* Washington, D.C.: U.S. Government Printing Office, 1977.

Discussion Questions

1. How effective do you think AFDC is in reducing the overall poverty rate? There has been a reduction in the number of people on the AFDC rolls since 1981, but there has also been a substantial increase in the poverty population. Explain.
2. OASDI, unemployment insurance, and AFDC reduce poverty and alleviate deprivation. Compare the strengths and weaknesses of the approaches underlying each of these programs as part of concerted antipoverty measures.
3. Less than 1 percent of total national income distributed among the poor would raise them all to the poverty threshold and thus alleviate poverty. If it appears that the price tag is so low, why hasn't the United States taken the necessary steps to eradicate poverty?
4. Why do you think there are separate veterans' programs based on needs tests?
5. "The negative income tax is the most efficient and equitable means of dealing with the poverty problem in the United States. With such a scheme, most welfare programs would become unnecessary." Explain.
6. Examine the trends and empirical data bearing on the thesis that there has been a growing interdependence between work and income maintenance. Outline the major ingredients of an income support policy that would do the least damage to work incentives.

3. Provision of Services and Goods

*For I was hungry and you gave me food, I was thirsty and you gave
me drink, I was a stranger and you welcomed me, I was naked and
you clothed me, I was sick and you visited me, I was in prison and
you came to me.*   —Matthew 25:35–36

The provision of goods and services complements cash assistance
to the poor. Although income support programs grew rapidly in the
late 1960s and early 1970s, efforts on behalf of the poor in the
following decade were dominated by in-kind assistance. Goods
and services accounted for nearly three-fifths of total federal outlays in aid of the poor in 1984, as compared with one-fifth of such
outlays in 1964 (figure 9). As a result, the welfare system has
assumed unprecedented scope and diversity, providing both necessities—such as medical care, food, and shelter—and supportive
services designed to improve the quality of life of poor people.

The heavy reliance on goods and services in antipoverty programs can be traced to a deep and longstanding public skepticism
concerning the moral character and reliability of poor people. In its
most cynical form, this skepticism is expressed in a view of the
poor as lazy and dishonest, beating the system and thriving on
government handouts. Those less suspicious often question the
ability of the poor to manage their own resources responsibly and
prefer providing goods and services that meet needs directly over
giving cash that the poor might squander. These perceptions of the
poor enhance the political acceptability of in-kind assistance that
appears to minimize the risk of fraud or waste. But even those who
favor maximum flexibility for the poor through direct income
support find that, in the absence of government intervention,
needed services and facilities are not available to the poor either
because of their isolation or because of shortcomings in market
mechanisms.

The relative merits of cash and in-kind assistance can be debated
at length, but it is important to note that the federal provision of
goods and services does offer some flexibility for the poor. While
some services (for example, compensatory education) are provided
directly by the government, many others are offered through a
system of payments and reimbursements that utilizes a broad range

Figure 9. Per capita cash and in-kind assistance for the poor (1984 dollars)

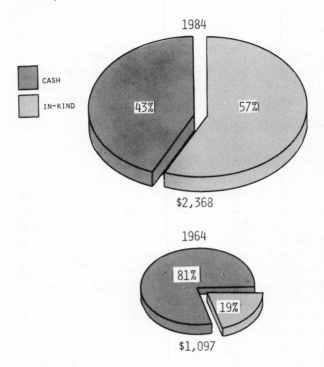

of service providers. Most health care for the poor is provided indirectly, with all three levels of government sharing the cost and with some opportunity for the poor to choose their own physicians rather than depending solely on care available in public institutions. By covering the cost of specific goods and services, these payments differ significantly from general income supplements, yet they allow more freedom of choice than the direct government provision of basic necessities.

As part of an overview of programs in aid of the poor, this chapter focuses primarily on goods and services made available by the federal government on the basis of need. A broader study would show that the federal role in the provision of goods and services extends far beyond these antipoverty efforts. The bulk of federal in-kind assistance is dispensed without regard to the recipients' level of income, at a cost far higher than federal expenditures expressly designed for the poor. For example, educating the nation's children and young adults alone costs twice as much as all federal programs targeted directly at the poor. The magnitude of aid to the nonpoor is illustrated even more clearly in what the late Richard M. Titmuss called the "iceberg phenomenon of social welfare," the revenue system that exempts certain types of expenditures from income taxes. (The provision allowing homeowners to deduct interest on home mortgages from taxable income is a typical example.) Therefore, even in the context of a discussion of those goods and services directed to the poor, it must be recognized that many direct public services—as well as "fiscal welfare" provisions—tend to favor the affluent members of society over the poor.

Medical Services

The linkage between poverty and poor health has long been recognized, and medical services are now considered to be an essential ingredient of even a minimum standard of living. Since the passage of medicare and medicaid in 1965, the federal government has assumed the major responsibility as the provider of health care for the aged and the poor. The estimated 1984 federal contribution to health care programs in aid of the poor totaled nearly $24 billion.

Estimated federal outlays for services to the poor

	(Millions)
Total	$23,912
Medicare	8,793
Medicaid	13,458
Community health projects	331
Veterans	700
Maternal and child health	218
Indians	412

Note: The total figure differs from others cited in the text because of different sources and methods of estimating the data. No exact figures are available.

Despite these massive public expenditures, the deficit in health care for the poor remains startling, whether measured in life expectancy, infant mortality rates, or numbers of visits to physicians or dentists. Considering the expanding government outlays, what accounts for the deficiencies in health care? No doubt some of the funds are wasted by inept administration. As in other areas, the health costs of the poor are also higher, especially when the government foots the bill. However, waste and overcharges reflect only part of the reason for soaring federal expenditures in health care and slow rates of health improvement. The following factors account for the persisting health deficiencies of the poor, and suggest that rapid improvements at a reasonable cost may remain elusive.

1. The poor, on the average, require more medical attention than the general population, a reflection of the very health conditions (advanced age, or physical or mental handicaps) that keep many of them out of the work force and prevent them from securing adequate incomes.

2. Preventive health care among the poor is typically inadequate. In addition to the nutritional deficiencies and environmental health risks facing the poor, the subsidized health care system itself encourages delay in treatment of health problems until they develop into major crises. Although recent extensions of medicaid coverage to most poor pregnant women and all poor children under age 5 suggest an increasing commitment to preventive health care, federal funds for the health care of poor children remain extremely limited.

3. The delivery system for health services, generally inefficient in America, is particularly disorganized and inadequate in serving the poor. Shortages of medical and allied health personnel have retarded the development of adequate health services in neighborhoods where economic incentives are limited, and yet the alternative of community health services is usually fragmented and often inaccessible.

Medicare and Medicaid

The federal government's most important health care programs are medicare and medicaid, both added to the Social Security Act in 1965. Medicare covers most hospital and medical costs for persons who are 65 years of age and older, as well as for disabled social security beneficiaries. Medicare is a universal program designed to help the elderly regardless of their income; about 10 percent of medicare outlays benefit the elderly poor. No doubt the medicare program has kept many near-poor elderly out of poverty, and has eased the anxieties of elderly persons whose life savings would have been wiped out as the result of a major illness. Of more direct benefit to the poor is medicaid, which provides health care coverage to persons receiving federally supported public assistance in all states except Arizona. Thirty-four states also extend medicaid eligibility to persons who do not qualify for public assistance but whose income is sufficiently low to quality them as "medically needy."

The medicare program offers elderly and disabled Americans both basic hospital insurance (Part A) and optional supplementary medical insurance (Part B). Hospital insurance pays a major part of costs for up to 90 days of hospitalization, as well as post-hospital extended care and home health services, for all social security and railroad retirement recipients and others who meet special qualifications such as workers and their dependents who need kidney transplantation or dialysis. These groups, as well as retired federal employees, can also choose to participate in the supplementary medical insurance program, which helps pay the cost of physicians' fees, diagnostic tests, medical supplies, and prescription drugs. Those enrolled in the supplementary program must pay a $14.60 monthly premium that is matched by the federal government. In 1984, 27.4 million aged and 3 million disabled persons were covered by hospital insurance and about 7.5 million were admitted to hospitals under Part A, while 20.3 million persons— two-thirds of those eligible—were enrolled in the supplementary program.

Medicaid was launched in 1965 to replace a fragmented and grossly inadequate system of medical assistance to recipients of separate public assistance programs. It offers reimbursements to states for a portion of the medical costs of low-income persons, about 80 percent of whom are recipients of either public assistance or SSI. The federal share of expenses ranges from 50 to 83 percent, depending upon the scope of services and eligibility requirements. Each state administers and operates its own programs, establishing its own rules within the confines of federal guidelines and regulations. In 1984, the federal contribution to medical services for 22 million low-income persons via medicaid totaled $20.3 billion, two-thirds of which aided persons below the poverty threshold. Despite medicare benefits, persons over 65 years of age continue to receive a larger portion of medicaid funds than any other recipient group (figure 10).

The dominant theme in the development of both medicare and medicaid programs—as well as in-kind assistance programs in shelter, food, and social services—has been the attempt to contain program costs. In the early stages of these programs, efforts to improve the quality of medical services for the elderly and poor led to federal requirements that states set standards for the reimbursement of hospitals and physicians at prevailing local rates. In order to allay fears of "socialized medicine," however, no provision was made for federal monitoring of reimbursements, and charges of

Figure 10. Medicaid, 1983

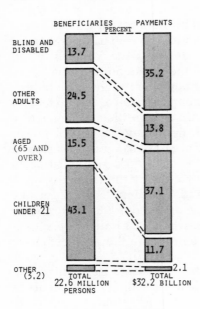

Source: U.S. Department of Health and Human Services

program fraud haunted both medicare and medicaid. In the early 1970s, Congress responded by directing federal administrators in charge of the program to spell out standards controlling the reimbursement of hospitals and physicians under medicare, medicaid, and maternal and child health programs. Self-regulation remained virtually in effect, however, leaving the administration of medicaid and other federal health care programs loosely monitored.

As the costs of federal health programs continued to soar in the 1970s, Congress experimented with various mechanisms to restrict further increases and to prevent fraud and abuse. In 1972 professional standards review organizations (PSROs) composed of local practitioners were established to monitor medicare and medicaid services. The PSROs, which did not begin functioning throughout the country until 1977, had neither the authority nor the will to contain hospital cost increases and therefore fell far short of their original aim. The concept of voluntary peer oversight has been preserved in modified peer review organizations (PROs), physician-sponsored or physician-assisted entities created in 1983 to review the medical necessity and quality of hospital services. Yet there is no reason to believe that the PROs will fare any better than their predecessors in restraining federal health care cost increases.

Attempts to halt rising federal health care expenditures have acquired a new sense of urgency in recent years in light of an impending financial crisis within medicare. The hospital insurance trust fund (Part A of medicare), financed through the social security payroll tax rather than general revenues, has been rapidly depleted by health care cost increases. According to 1984 projections of payroll tax revenues and hospital insurance outlays, Part A will reach bankruptcy by the end of the decade unless Congress adopts effective medicare reforms. Because both payroll tax hikes and medicare benefit cuts will prove politically difficult, proposals to shore up the hospital insurance trust fund have increasingly focused upon mechanisms for stemming future increases in health care costs.

The Reagan administration has taken some halting steps toward federal control of health care costs through changes in medicare payments for hospital services. In 1982, limits were placed on medicare reimbursements to hospitals with above-average costs, and during 1983 a more comprehensive system of "prospective reimbursement" was established that sets maximum hospital charges for services to medicare patients. The intent of prospective reimbursement is to give hospitals a financial incentive to hold down medical costs, forcing them to absorb the loss if their actual costs exceed federally established reimbursement rates but also allowing them to reap savings when covered services cost less than the medicare standard. While this reliance upon financial incentives bears some resemblance to market mechanisms, the Reagan administration markedly increased federal regulation of the health care industry by taking the authority to set rates for medicare services away from hospital administrators and placing it in the hands of federal bureaucrats.

Because the supplementary medical insurance program (Part B) is financed through premiums and general revenues, the burden of rising health care expenditures in this component of medicare has fallen directly on both participants and the federal government. In an attempt to restrict federal outlays under Part B, the Reagan administration has shifted additional medical costs onto those enrolled in the program. Monthly premiums for supplementary medical insurance increased by 45 percent between 1981 and 1984, and the Reagan administration proposed in fiscal 1985 to raise participants' contributions further by doubling the monthly premium in a single year. If the Reagan proposals had been accepted by Congress, recipients' out-of-pocket costs under Part B (including deductibles) would have jumped from $250 to $510 per year before medicare reimbursements became available.

The Reagan administration's policy has renewed concerns that rising premium costs and deductibles in the supplementary medical insurance program will discourage many aged near-poor from participating. In addition to the monthly premium and $75 annual deductible, the enrollee is responsible for 20 percent of all remaining costs. States are required to pay premiums, deductibles, and the 20 percent of uncovered costs for elderly persons receiving supplementary security income payments. People who are deemed "medically needy"—those whose incomes are barely above the poverty threshold—must pay their own premiums, although states may pay deductibles and additional out-of-pocket costs. However, only a relatively few states and the District of Columbia provide these benefits for their elderly medically needy population.

Finally, the Reagan administration has responded to increasing medicaid expenditures by restricting coverage and benefits for working families near the poverty line. Because states establish their own eligibility requirements under medicaid, the impact of federal budget cuts in the early 1980s has varied across jurisdictions. Yet reductions in federal outlays, combined with fiscal pressures at the state level, caused 40 states to adopt cuts in medicaid benefits in 1981 and 30 states to enact further reductions in 1982. The Reagan administration's restrictions in AFDC eligibility also undermined medicaid coverage for the near-poor, as those forced off the AFDC rolls in many states automatically lost medicaid benefits as well. Although Congress in 1984 restored federal funding for medicaid to its 1981 levels, it is not clear whether states will use these additional funds to restore medicaid services cut in previous years or simply keep them as windfall savings for their state treasuries.

Increases in federal outlays for medicare and medicaid are likely to fuel continued debate over rising health care costs for the remainder of this decade. The growing cost of federal health programs since the mid 1970s can be traced in large part to the reluctance of Congress to restrict overall increases in hospital revenues and expenditures. The Carter administration championed a broad hospital cost containment measure in 1978 and 1979, but the legislation was defeated in Congress after intense lobbying by the hospital industry and medical associations. Whether an acceptable framework for restraining hospital costs can be developed in the 1980s is unclear, but in the absence of such an initiative it will remain exceedingly difficult to reconcile the goals of affordability and adequate health care coverage in the medicare and medicaid programs.

Community, Maternal, and Child Health

In addition to health insurance for the poor, federal programs have sought to improve the quality and efficiency of health care services to the poor. Under the Great Society, the assumption that improving the health of the poor required not only massive funds but also a major restructuring of the health care delivery system led to the creation of community health centers in low-income areas. These federally funded neighborhood health centers were established to fulfill four basic goals: (1) to provide a full range of ambulatory health services; (2) to maintain a close liaison with other community services; (3) to develop close working relationships with a hospital (preferably one with a medical school affiliation); and (4) to foster the participation of the indigenous population in decisionmaking and employment in the centers. By restructuring the health care system in poor neighborhoods and supplementing the services of private physicians, the neighborhood health centers provided an essential complement to insurance coverage in federal health care policy. Federal support for community health centers has continued long after the dismantling of the Office of Economic Opportunity, the antipoverty agency under which the centers were first created. Despite the Reagan administration's efforts to consolidate federal health care programs in 1981, Congress ensured that funding for the health centers would be preserved by creating a separate block grant to states for primary health care provided through community health centers. However, compared with other government contributions to medical services for the poor, outlays for health centers have constituted little more than a drop in the bucket, and even that federal funding was reduced by 23 percent during the Reagan administration. Outlays for the primary care block grant totaled $331 million in 1984.

During the 1970s, numerous categorical programs were also launched by Congress in attempts to bolster maternal and child health in low-income families. These diverse initiatives— including programs to reduce infant mortality and childhood disability, to provide rehabilitative services for blind and disabled children, to furnish treatment and care to crippled children, and to provide other prenatal and children's health services—were consolidated into a single block grant to states in 1981 at reduced funding levels. In order to compensate for a 17 percent reduction in federal funds under the Reagan administration, the great majority of states were forced to curtail prenatal and delivery services to low-income women in the early 1980s. Ironically, it is particularly in the areas of maternal and child health that federal funds can have their greatest preventive impact, diminishing the likelihood of future health problems for both mothers and infants while increasing the chances for full physical and mental development among poor children.

Veterans

A variety of other programs provide subsidized health care for the poor, most of them concentrating on specific groups—Indians, veterans, migrants, or handicapped children. The most extensive of these are the medical programs for veterans.

The Veterans Administration health care system, originally designed to care for war wounded, currently provides free care on a broad scale to aged and indigent veterans whether or not their medical needs are related to military service. All "medically indigent" war veterans are eligible for VA hospital care, and most of the patients in VA hospitals have no service-connected injury. The criteria for eligibility are based not on established income limitations, but rather on the veterans' perception of their ability to purchase medical care.

The VA spent $8.1 billion on medical care in 1984. The system operates 172 hospitals, 101 nursing homes, 16 domiciliaries, and 225 outpatient clinics. The VA also contributes to the cost of care received by veterans in state-run domiciliaries and nursing homes. Due to the aging of the veteran population, the demand for nursing home beds is sure to increase in the 1980s and beyond. In 1984 there were 4 million veterans over age 65, but by 1990 this number is projected to nearly double with veterans constituting one-half of the aged male population. Since veterans are automatically eligible for free health care after they turn 65, the increase of aging veterans could double VA medical expenditures by the end of the decade.

In considering the impact of the VA health care system in aiding the poor, the parallels between the VA and medicare programs are striking. By using eligibility criteria not strictly related to poverty, both health care programs fail to bring aid efficiently to the most needy. Yet even in the absence of a highly targeted program structure, many of the aged served by medicare and the veterans served by the VA system are indeed poor or would be impoverished by medical costs. With the recognition that both programs also serve as "safety nets" that keep the near-poor from economic disaster when costly illness strikes, the case for using VA and medicare programs as vehicles for aid to the poor becomes, if not persuasive, at least more understandable.

Native Americans

The American Indian living on a reservation and the Alaskan native are perhaps the most poverty-stricken minorities in the country, yet the American health care system offers these groups only limited relief. About one-half of all American Indians live on isolated reservations and most native Alaskans reside in inland villages; such geographic and economic settings rarely attract private health facilities. Poor roads and inadequate transportation and communication heighten these barriers to health care, creating serious problems for individuals hampered by illness. Although Native Americans are eligible for medicaid, even its impact is diminished by geographic location—about one-fourth of the reservation population resides in Arizona, the only state not participating in medicaid programs.

In this context, it is clear that both isolation and poverty take their tolls. The incidence of tuberculosis is three times greater among Indians than the rest of the population, and Indians also suffer disproportionately from streptococcal infections, nutritional and dental deficiencies, poor mental health, and attendant disorders. Alaskan natives fare only slightly better in major health indices. It is this dramatic result of isolation and poverty that created a mandate for special health services under the auspices of the U.S. Department of Health and Human Services.

The Indian Health Service (IHS) meets some of these medical needs, employing some 11,400 health service personnel in the 47 hospitals, 84 health centers, and 300 smaller health stations and satellite clinics that it operates. There are also four hospitals and more than 250 clinics that are operated by tribes under contract with the IHS, in addition to contracted services with nonfederal facilities. The expenditures by the IHS for maintaining these services and facilities amounted to $692 million in 1983.

Measured in terms of progress in lessening the tremendous health deficit of Indians, the efforts of the Indian Health Service over recent decades have resulted in considerable progress. For example, since 1955, the life expectancy of Indians has increased several years. Moreover, the Indian death rate from influenza and pneumonia decreased 73 percent, the maternal death rate declined 86 percent, and death from tuberculosis dropped 94 percent. The infant mortality rate has also declined from 61 to 15 deaths per

1,000 live births. Family-planning services are supplied to a growing portion of the female population between 15 and 44 years of
age; consequently, the annual birth rate per 1,000 people has
dropped from 37 to 31 births.

Despite the progress achieved under the Indian Health Service,
facilities remain primitive compared with sophisticated city hospitals, and the service lacks adequate and experienced personnel.
In order to alleviate shortages of physicians and other health care
personnel, as well as to eliminate the cultural gaps between the
health workers and the target population, IHS has pushed for more
extensive training of Indian health personnel. The Indian health
manpower program recruits Indians to pursue health careers and
offers professional scholarships to those who choose to study in the
health field. In order to improve the health of the Native American
population, underlying deficiencies in housing, nutrition, and
health education must also be corrected.

Shelter

Given the high and rising cost of shelter, both old and new, poor
families are faced with grim choices: they can live in substandard
units, they can crowd into better dwellings, or they can use a
disproportionate share of their meager incomes for housing. In
many cases, they must resort to all three. Of the 1981 year-round
housing stock of 89.6 million units, 2.4 million lacked plumbing
facilities and as many as several million were dilapidated and in
need of major repairs. In the same year, there were over 3.6 million
occupied units with more than one person per room—the accepted
American standard for overcrowding. While average Americans
spend 17 percent of their income for rent or home ownership costs
and an additional 5 percent for furnishings and equipment, the
relative burdens of the poor are considerably greater. Close to half
of all renter families had to spend more than 25 percent of their
income for shelter and utilities, and one-third paid over 35 percent.

Various federal policies have been enacted to help alleviate the
nation's housing problems. Programs that subsidize the construction, rental, leasing, purchase, and operation of apartments
and houses for low-income households are of greatest importance
to the poor. At the end of 1983, 3.8 million households were
receiving housing assistance through either the U.S. Department of
Housing and Urban Development or the U.S. Department of Agriculture, with annual subsidies exceeding $10 billion. Federal
loan programs and tax expenditures also provide broader as-

sistance for housing construction and purchases, thereby enhancing the nation's overall housing stock.

Public Housing

Initiated in 1937 and currently serving 1.3 million households, public housing is the oldest and one of the largest housing assistance programs for the poor. The public housing program provides federal subsidies for the amortization of construction costs on units built, owned, and operated by local public housing authorities (PHAs). The units are reserved for low-income families, with locally established income limits that cannot exceed 80 percent of the median income level in the area. For the most part, however, eligibility is restricted to households with yearly incomes below 50 percent of the median income. Less than 10 percent of the units are available to households with incomes between 50 and 80 percent of the area median; the remainder are reserved for very low income households. Given the eligibility restrictions, the average public housing household has an income of 30 percent of the area median.

Originally, the federal subsidy for public housing was only to cover capital costs, with rents covering the operating expenses. As operating costs continued to rise, however, poor households could not pay the rent necessary to cover operating costs fully. Consequently, in 1969 federal law authorized subsidy payments to make up the difference between operating costs and tenants' ability to pay, defined as 30 percent of a household's adjusted income. In 1984 a total of 1.3 million existing public housing units required an annual operating subsidy of $1,140 per unit.

From the inception of direct federal housing aid during the 1930s until the advent of rent subsidies during the Great Society, public housing was the mainstay of efforts to ensure shelter for the poor. Even throughout the 1970s and on into the 1980s, public housing brought highly targeted assistance to the poor, often working in tandem with other public assistance programs. Of the occupants in public housing, three families in five receive some form of welfare income. Three-fourths of family households in public housing are minorities, with 60 percent black and 15 percent Hispanic. Persons aged 62 and over occupy 45 percent of the units, and the gross annual income for all families residing in public housing averaged about $6,300.

The greatest strength of public housing—its highly targeted aid to the poor—has also generated the program's greatest political liability. As became apparent in the 1960s, the construction and operation of housing for low-income families is a massive under-taking that can be very expensive. In 1984 the estimated average construction cost for a new unit of public housing, authorized prior to the Reagan administration, was $56,500, with an average annual federal subsidy for construction and financing of approximately $5,000 per unit.

Despite its long history, public housing has been plagued by increasing difficulties over the past decade. To save costs and to avoid political opposition, many public housing units were lo-cated in large-scale, inner-city projects. Yet the concentration of poor families in deteriorating neighborhoods often led to problems of vandalism, crime, and general malaise among tenants. Many central city housing authorities proved unable to maintain their units in the face of such widespread problems, and public oppo-sition frequently forestalled the initiation of new projects. Finally, rising construction and operating costs undermined political sup-port for public housing, causing federal investments to decline. The Reagan administration has placed greater reliance on the stock of existing housing to meet public housing needs, rather than investing in more costly new construction projects. However, long waiting lists for public housing projects still attest that the poor have few alternatives for decent shelter.

Subsidized Housing

New approaches to the housing needs of the poor that relied upon the leasing of private units by local housing authorities or the provision of rent supplements directly to low-income families were first tested in the 1960s. In experimenting with these subsidy and incentive programs, critics of public housing hoped to dis-perse low-income families beyond the confines of neighborhoods with a high concentration of poverty and to contain federal housing costs by relying on existing housing stock. Neither approach yielded much success in dispersing low-income families. In the absence of suburban cooperation, the overwhelming majority of leased units remain in low-income neighborhoods. Rent supplements may have had more potential for promoting dispersal, but the sky-rocketing operating costs of other federally assisted housing have forced a "piggybacking" of rent supplements with other housing subsidies to keep rent levels within the reach of low-income households. Thus, most of the units covered under the rent sup-plement program were in completely rent-supplemented projects, or were used along with other subsidy programs to reach an even lower-income clientele.

The most significant rent supplement program was established by Section 8 of the Housing and Community Development Act of 1974. The law offers communities greater opportunity to shape federal block grant aid to match local conditions and needs and provides recipients of rent subsidies a choice of location and housing type in publicly or privately owned units. Section 8 provides no direct assistance for either construction or permanent financing, but indirect aid in financing may be obtained through state housing finance agencies or local public housing authorities. From 1970 to 1981, subsidized housing outlays grew at an annual rate of 18.2 percent, but growth has slowed sharply under the Reagan administration.

Households with incomes below 80 percent of the median in their area, or 200 percent of the national poverty line, are eligible for Section 8 assistance. Those with incomes under 50 percent of the area median pay between 20 and 25 percent of their income in rent, and those with slightly higher incomes can be required to pay up to a maximum of 30 percent of their incomes. Beginning in October 1985, however, the established rent for all tenants will be changed to the higher of 30 percent of adjusted income or 10 percent of gross income. The federal government pays the difference between the tenant's payment and the actual rental. Section 8 housing is becoming more highly targeted to the poor, as 95 percent of all new participants must have incomes of less than 50 percent of the area median.

Subsidized housing grew rapidly under Section 8 during the late 1970s, reaching a peak when one-fourth of all renters below the poverty line lived in subsidized housing. Despite slow growth in the 1980s, the Section 8 program, after just a decade of operation, has overtaken public housing as the major federal program offering housing assistance to the poor. At the same time, however, the federal government has substantially reduced its commitment to supporting construction of lower-income housing. Because the cost of new construction is approximately three times as great as the cost of maintaining existing structures, Congress has repealed the authority to make new commitments in the Section 8 construction program, except for units built with housing loans for the elderly.

In 1983 Congress enacted two alternative programs to improve the housing situation of the poor. Rental rehabilitation grants help states and localities rehabilitate properties for low-income renters. The federal government may subsidize up to one-half the cost of rehabilitating approximately 30,000 rental housing units per year.

In addition, the Housing Urban-Rural Recovery Act authorized the construction or substantial rehabilitation of rental housing in low- and moderate-income neighborhoods with a shortage of rental housing. The 1985 appropriations for these programs amounted to $95 million.

In retrospect, the Housing and Community Development Act of 1974 represented a departure from establishment of a national housing policy. By stressing community block grants that could be spent by local officials according to broad guidelines, Congress substituted local discretion for a strong federal role in providing housing for the poor. Although the 1949 pledge of "a decent home and suitable living environment for every American family" has not been formally abandoned, inflationary trends and rising housing costs have reversed the earlier gains of federal housing policy. The emphasis in housing—as in other social action areas—is on returning the strategy initiative to the local level. Whether community officials will continue to make optimal use of the federal dollar remains to be seen.

The federal government continues to provide broader incentives and financial support to promote the construction of new homes for middle-income families, thereby hoping to open vacancies for lower-income renters and home buyers. Roughly 18 percent of all mortgage loans for private homes are guaranteed by the Federal Housing Administration, the Veterans Administration, or the Farmers Home Administration. Savings to homeowners and rental property owners from special tax treatment amounted to $23 billion in 1984. All these forms of assistance stimulate housing construction, and while the poor receive only a minute proportion of this aid, the benefits may "trickle down" to them. Federal incentives and aids for new construction contributed to the more than 80 percent decline in substandard housing between 1960 and 1981.

Aside from assuming a direct financial burden, Congress has taken legislative action beyond the open housing laws in attempting to alter the structural elements of the housing market itself. Although as yet unwilling to outlaw "redlining"—the practice of refusing to make loans in certain urban neighborhoods regardless of personal creditworthiness—the Congress did enact legislation in 1975 to discourage the practice by forcing lending institutions to disclose the amounts of mortgage money they lend to different areas of a city. During the Carter administration, the Department of Housing and Urban Development also adopted a more aggressive role by challenging in the courts the exclusionary zoning policies of affluent communities, as well as by monitoring local compliance with federal equal opportunity housing statutes as a condition for receipt of federal community development and recreation funds. The Reagan administration has largely reversed this trend, returning to a passive role of processing individual housing discrimination complaints while initiating no action to discourage more pervasive patterns of development that yield discriminatory results. Yet without altering these basic patterns, even massive infusion of federal funds through existing housing programs can do little to promote the dispersal of low-income units that is so vital to the future of the poor.

Household Energy

Fuel and weatherization assistance for low-income households represents a relatively new extension of the welfare system. Policies designed to help the poor heat their homes were initiated in response to rising fuel costs—a problem aggravated by President Carter's 1979 decision to decontrol the price of domestic oil—and reflect an expanded concept of basic needs. During the first decade following the initial OPEC cartel boost of oil prices, the real cost of fuel nearly quintupled. In 1970, home energy costs accounted for 9 percent of the entire income for low-income households and about 3 percent for the average American household. By 1984, home energy costs for low-income households represented about twenty-five percent of their income, three to four times the share paid by the average American household.

The low-income energy assistance program (LIEAP) was initiated in 1978 as an experimental effort and made permanent in 1980. Administered by the Department of Health and Human Services, the program distributes block grants to the states, the amount depending on the climate and the number of low-income households in each state. Funds are used to cover the residential heating or cooling costs of the poor and near-poor, to purchase and/or install low-cost weatherization materials, and to help households with energy-related emergency situations. States may use a maximum of 15 percent of their funds for weatherization activities and can also transfer up to 10 percent of allotments to other block grants. Funding for fiscal 1985 was set at almost $1.9 billion, which represents a slight decline from levels in the early 1980s.

Eligibility for LIEAP is granted to households receiving AFDC, SSI, food stamps, or certain veterans' assistance, or to any household that has an income below either 150 percent of the poverty line or 60 percent of a state's standard of need, whichever is higher. The Department of Health and Human Services has estimated that approximately 21 million households meet these eligibility limits.

Since 1975 federal programs have also helped low-income households conserve energy. Families with incomes below 125 percent of the poverty threshold or who received AFDC, SSI, or general assistance within the last 12 months are eligible for assistance. The Department of Energy allocates weatherization funds to the states based on a formula that considers local temperatures and heating requirements, along with estimated numbers of low-income households. In 1985 the maximum weatherization grant per dwelling was $1,600.

Food

A federal role in the provision of food to the poor has been acknowledged for little more than two decades. Although the federal food stamp program was in operation nationally from 1939 to 1943, the program was not revived as a source of in-kind aid to the poor until 1961. Similarly, the diverse child nutrition programs were not launched until the Great Society era of the 1960s with the establishment of the school lunch, school breakfast, and special milk programs. Yet, after a slow beginning in the 1960s, federal spending for food assistance to the poor grew rapidly, reaching a total of $17.7 billion by 1984. The major components of the program included food stamps, child and elderly nutrition, and distribution of surplus food (figure 11).

This dramatic expansion of food programs was the result of a highly diverse political coalition with widely varying interests and concerns. Some saw food programs as a way of getting more for the poor by raising the cry of "hunger in America." Others favored food distribution because they were concerned that the poor would use cash grants unwisely. Still others sought to sustain the demand for certain agricultural products. Yet the result was a strong and repeated public policy preference for providing food directly to the poor instead of allocating a portion of their cash assistance to food, and a corresponding growth in the federal network of in-kind assistance programs. Over 90 percent of all benefits under these food programs are distributed on the basis of need, and perhaps more than in any other in-kind aid program the poor, including the working poor, receive an overwhelming share of this federal assistance.

Figure 11. Food Assistance, 1972, 1980, and 1984

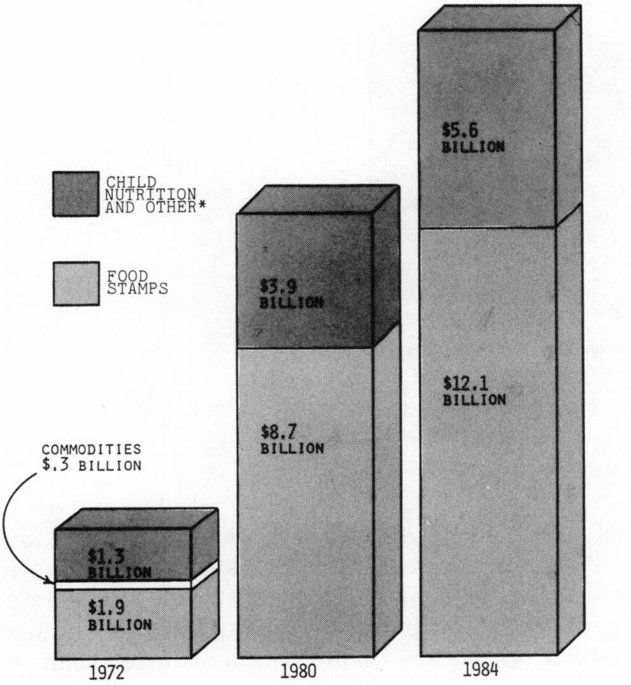

CHILD
NUTRITION
AND OTHER*

FOOD
STAMPS

$5.6
BILLION

$3.9
BILLION

$12.1
BILLION

$8.7
BILLION

COMMODITIES
$.3 BILLION

$1.3
BILLION

$1.9
BILLION

1972   1980   1984

*Includes nutrition for elderly and commodity distribution.

Source: Budget of the United States Government, Fiscal 1985

Food Stamps

By far the largest of federal food subsidies, the food stamp program is designed to increase the purchasing power of an estimated 21.6 million persons at a cost in 1984 of $12.1 billion (figure 12). Under this program, households receive monthly allotments of food stamps based on their income and household size. Although recipients would undoubtedly find cash easier and less demeaning to use, food stamps may be used in retail stores to purchase any food for human consumption except alcoholic beverages, tobacco, and imported food (no Russian caviar).

The food stamp program is open to all public assistance recipients except supplemental security income recipients in states that provide food stamp benefits in the form of increased SSI

Figure 12. Food stamp program cost and participation

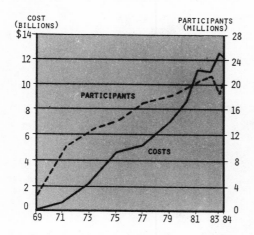

Source: Budget of the United States Government, Fiscal 1985

payments. Other households with net incomes at or below the poverty level, after certain allowable deductions are subtracted, are also eligible. In 1984 an estimated 95 percent of all food stamp recipients had gross incomes (before any deductions) below the poverty level. About 40 percent of the recipients also received public assistance, 20 percent were SSI recipients, and 26 percent were receiving social security, disability, or retirement income.

In 1984 the maximum monthly food stamp allotment for a family of four was $264, equal to the Department of Agriculture's Thrifty Food Plan of 73 cents per meal for each person. This amount was reduced by 30 percent of a household's net income (after certain allowable deductions) based on the assumption, similar to that used in calculating the poverty threshold, that a family spent 30 percent of its income on food. This allowed a family of four with a monthly income of $675 to receive $90 in food stamps per month ($675 less a $95 standard deduction and 30 percent of the remainder subtracted from the maximum of $264). In 1984 the average food stamp benefit was 47 cents per person per meal. Benefit levels are adjusted periodically to reflect changes in food prices. The food stamp allotment is supposed to enable a family to maintain what the Department of Agriculture calls a "nutritionally adequate" diet, but this regimen requires nutritional planning skills, storage space, equipment, and low-cost markets, resources infrequently available to the poor.

The food stamp program is jointly operated by the federal and state governments and is available in all states. The federal government finances the direct cost of food stamps and a share of state program administrative costs. The responsibility for program administration and the distribution of food stamps is left to each state.

After a slow start in the 1960s, the program grew rapidly during the 1970s. While the expansion of food stamps in the 1970s paralleled the growth of cash welfare in the late 1960s, it also provided a subsidy to the working poor. Among the important factors were:

1. More generous benefits. Congress enacted generally higher benefits and removed obstacles to participation for the poorest families. In addition, benefits are adjusted annually by the increase in the cost of living.

2. Increased utilization. An increasing proportion of public assistance households, which are automatically eligible, availed themselves of benefits as a result of extensive media publicity and the outreach efforts of public and private groups.

3. High unemployment rates during the mid-1970s and early 1980s. The Agriculture Department estimated that each one percent rise in the unemployment rate might add about 600,000 additional participants.

By the late 1970s, record food stamp expenditures had prompted diverse attempts to contain burgeoning program costs. To ensure that aid is not channeled to the non-needy, numerous safeguards against fraud, abuse, and waste have been instituted by Congress. Regulatory requirements and financial incentives have been employed in efforts to improve state administration of the food stamp program, including reporting requirements to verify eligibility and bonus payments to states that maintain low rates of error. The federal government has also taken an increasingly aggressive role in investigating allegations of food stamp fraud and abuse. Charges of widespread fraud have never been substantiated, and while past administrative errors in determining eligibility and computing benefits have been a source of political frustration and embarrassment they have not added greatly to the overall number of food stamp recipients.

The concern that food stamps be restricted only to those who can not support themselves also led Congress to establish a work requirement for recipients. Except for persons with child-care responsibilities and persons already working, all able-bodied persons between 18 and 60 in households receiving food stamps must register for employment and accept suitable work paying the going rate in the locality, even though in some cases it may be below the federal minimum wage. States and localities also have the option to operate food stamp "workfare" programs where unemployed or underemployed able-bodied adult food stamp recipients not caring for dependents are required to "work off" their benefit in a public service job to retain eligibility. Because most food stamp recipients are either already working or not available for work, however, few states have extended the workfare concept to include the food stamp program.

Since 1977, Congress has imposed a spending cap on the food stamp program in a vain attempt to hold down costs without slashing benefit levels. In each year that food stamp expenditures have threatened to exceed the authorized aggregate ceiling, Congress has been faced with the choice of suspending benefits completely upon exhaustion of appropriated funds or approving supplemental expenditures sufficient to support benefits through the end of the fiscal year. Predictably, Congress has repeatedly opted for such last-minute extensions. Despite its ineffectiveness as a mechanism for restraining food stamp costs, the spending cap remains in federal law, set at a level of $13.9 billion in fiscal 1985.

The program has been successful in targeting benefits to those most in need and offering assistance to the working poor. Food stamp revisions enacted in 1977 contributed to this narrow focus by lowering income ceilings for eligibility while at the same time eliminating the "cash purchase" requirement that previously prevented some very poor households from participating in the program. According to the Agriculture Department, two out of every three food stamp households are headed by women, one of twelve recipients are elderly, and almost half of all recipients are children. In 1984, over two-fifths of participant households had gross incomes of less than $3,600, with an average gross income per household of $4,152.

Still, some families who would not normally be considered poor are beneficiaries of the program because various costs may be deducted from a family's gross income to compute eligibility and benefit amount. In addition to a $95 standard deduction (in 1984), allowance is also made for a deduction of 18 percent of earned income to make up for work-related expenses and social security and income taxes. Furthermore, a combined deduction of up to $134 is allowable for dependent care costs and/or excessive shelter costs. Though it is not common, a family of four with a gross annual income of $12,876 could be eligible to receive $69 in monthly food stamps by deducting a possible $422 a month, leaving a net income for food stamp purposes of $651 a month. The average monthly deduction claimed by food stamp families in 1984 was $141.

In attempting to focus food stamp aid very narrowly to the "truly needy," however, the Reagan administration has undermined the adequacy of benefit levels in the early 1980s. Under President Reagan's policies, nearly one million food stamp recipients became ineligible for benefits and virtually all others suffered real losses in food purchasing power. Although these budget cuts were intended primarily to restrict aid to the near-poor, roughly two-thirds of the spending reductions were achieved through benefit cuts for families below the poverty threshold. Deeper cuts in the food stamp program proposed by the Reagan administration in 1982 and 1983 would have reduced benefits for four out of every five of the poorest food stamp households—those with incomes of less than half the poverty standard—but this more radical proposal was rejected by Congress.

The importance of the food stamp program in the scope of federal antipoverty efforts is beyond dispute. Even while the program fails to meet the complete nutritional needs of recipients, it has improved the access of the poor to essential food supplies. Perhaps more important, the food stamp program remains one of the few federal initiatives that extends to the working poor. By so doing it preserves some sense of equity for that neglected segment of the welfare population.

Child Nutrition

Aside from the broad effort to use food stamps as a vehicle for aid to the American poor, federal food assistance has been sharply focused on the area of child nutrition. A variety of programs now provide breakfast, lunch, and milk to 24.6 million children in private and public schools and day care centers, at a federal cost in 1984 of $4.1 billion. Federal aid is provided through state agencies in the form of cash or commodities that subsidize nutritional meals for children, with special aid targeted at children from low-income families.

By far the largest of the food and nutrition programs is the school lunch program, with federal costs of $2.2 billion in fiscal 1984. About 23 million children, more than five in nine of the entire population, receive a subsidized lunch daily. Federal reimbursement is provided on the basis of all meals served, regardless of children's family income, and additional assistance is provided for meals served free or at reduced cost to children from poor or near-poor families. In 1984 about 10.4 million children from poor or near-poor homes received free meals at an average federal subsidy of $1.26 per meal, 1.5 million received reduced-price lunches at an average subsidy of 86 cents, and 11.3 million children received lunches at an average federal cost of 12 cents.

The school breakfast and special milk programs are smaller in scope, and yet they too have a significant impact on child nutrition. In 1983 federal outlays for these programs amounted to $365 million. Free or reduced-priced breakfasts were offered to 3.2 million children (mostly in schools in low-income areas), with a maximum subsidy of 76 cents per meal. Similarly, the special milk program provided added nourishment to over 1 million children in participating schools, institutions, and summer camps. In order to eliminate program overlap, only those schools that do not participate in other food and nutritional service programs are eligible for the special milk program.

Child nutrition programs reach outside the traditional school setting to provide in-kind aid in summer camps, day care centers, and local health clinics. About 1.4 million children benefit from the summer food program and 1 million children receive meals from the child care food program. Spending for these programs reached $433 million in fiscal 1983.

Finally, two additional programs—the special supplemental feeding program for women, infants, and children (WIC) and the commodity supplemental food program—channel aid to low-income, pregnant, and postpartum women, and infants and children up to age five whose inadequate diets may endanger their health. In 1984 an estimated 2.3 million persons participated in the two programs at a cost of $1.1 billion.

As in other areas, the Reagan administration succeeded in curtailing federal expenditures for child nutrition. Federal support for the school lunch program dropped by 30 percent in the early 1980s, resulting in a loss of roughly 3 million children from the program. Funding for the school breakfast program also declined by 20 percent under the Reagan administration, allowing it to reach some 500,000 fewer children in 1984 than in 1981. Finally, summer food programs not run by schools or local governments were terminated by President Reagan, eliminating aid to about 500,000 low-income children previously served by churches and other nonprofit private agencies when schools were not in session.

Perhaps the most disturbing aspect of the Reagan administration's school lunch cuts has been the complete withdrawal of numerous school systems from participation in the program. Even during the 1970s many children were denied access to school lunches because their schools did not have the necessary equipment or funds to meet federal matching requirements for operating expenses. This problem was particularly acute for schools in poor neighborhoods—schools serving those children most in need of nutrition benefits. Under more restrictive eligibility requirements in the early 1980s, additional schools have lost the economies of scale necessary to keep their school lunch programs afloat.

The school lunch and breakfast programs have yielded gains, but some serious flaws remain in serving the poor. For every two children who received free or reduced-priced lunches, at least one more child—perhaps several million altogether—was eligible but did not benefit. The process of establishing eligibility can be complicated for the applicant and can create a great deal of paperwork for the schools. Moreover, children who qualify for free or reduced-price lunches are often singled out by standing in separate lines, eating at specified tables, or using distinctive lunch tokens. The involved certification procedures and stigmatization of children may discourage many needy children from applying for free meals. While the advances brought by child nutrition programs since the mid-1960s are significant, their shortcomings underscore the special barriers that can accompany programs of indirect, in-kind assistance to the poor.

Social Services

As federal programs for the poor expanded during the 1960s, Congress increasingly acknowledged the importance of social services in helping the poor cope with their own lives and preserving some stability for future generations. The scope of social services is so broad as to defy definition; assistance ranges from narrow interventions, such as child and foster parent care, family planning, drug and alcohol abuse treatment, and legal aid, to broader forms such as counseling and referral services. Services to the mentally retarded and support programs for the elderly are also available. The mere process of identifying a problem, even if nothing can be done to relieve it, is regarded as a social service.

Federal support for social services is authorized under a social services block grant (SSBG) which consolidated the funding of several categorical programs. The 1981 provisions of the SSBG reflect the Reagan administration's desire to channel greater decision-making power to the states, eliminating a number of restrictions and requirements imposed upon federally funded social services under Title XX of the Social Security Act. For example, states are no longer required to provide a minimum level of services to public assistance recipients or adhere to federal income eligibility limits. States can now design their own mix of services, establish their own eligibility requirements, and allocate federal funds without providing matching funds from state treasuries.

One element that has remained strictly regulated by the federal government, however, is overall program cost. In order to counteract burgeoning federal social service expenditures, which reached $4 billion by 1972, Congress established a ceiling limiting such outlays to $2.5 billion annually. Subsequent Congresses slowly raised this spending cap to $2.9 billion by fiscal 1980, but federal outlays under SSBG have been brought down once again, with appropriations for fiscal 1985 set at $2.7 billion. This ceiling has successfully held social service costs well below growth rates in other federal in-kind assistance programs.

Changing Institutions

In virtually all federal in-kind assistance programs—medical services, shelter, food, and social services—the pattern of development throughout the 1960s and into the 1980s is strikingly uniform. The federal government in all of these programs responded to the relatively immediate needs of the poor, demonstrated a consistent preference for in-kind rather than cash aid, and ultimately searched for ways to control costs as federal outlays ballooned. Yet in one unique federal initiative—community action—the goals and philosophy were markedly different. In struggling with its distinctive role in federal antipoverty efforts, the community action approach carved a history all its own.

Arising out of President Johnson's antipoverty initiatives in the mid-1960s, the community action experiment tested a bold, unprecedented approach to the problems of the poor. Rather than responding to the immediate needs of Americans in poverty, or even to the long-range personal barriers to individual advancement (for example, lack of education and training or the need for family planning), community action embraced the ambitious goal of structural and institutional change in an attempt to alter some of the fundamental social, political, and economic forces that trapped the poor in poverty. Unlike other federal programs in aid of the poor, the goal of community action was not simply to raise the effective income of the poor, it was to change the very situation keeping millions of Americans below the poverty threshold each year.

The structure of community action efforts was carefully drafted in response to the lessons of more traditional antipoverty programs. The architects of the Great Society recognized that the federal bureaucracy was far removed from the needs and realities of the populations it served, and that the tradition of grudging and paternal assistance contributed little to individual self-esteem or to the collective abilities of the poor. As an alternative, the Johnson administration sought a strategy for fighting poverty that required the participation of the poor in the design and operation of the programs that served them. By attempting to involve the poor in the decision-making process, including the choice of services and delivery systems, the intent was to promote as much discretion and innovation as possible at the local level. Ultimately, three primary vehicles for this new approach emerged: the community action program (CAP), legal services, and the community development corporations.

The community action program was a product of the Great Society's Economic Opportunity Act of 1964. It funded the establishment of almost 1,000 community based agencies in urban neighborhoods, rural areas, and on Indian reservations. The poor were represented on their planning boards and in many cases were hired to help operate the programs. The community agencies quickly became a catch-all for projects aiding the poor, acting as sponsors for a variety of social programs funded by federal, state, local and private agencies. Yet their primary goal continued to be the development of mechanisms through which the poor could make their needs known to local government officials, civic organizations, employers, and labor interests who were in a position to offer direct local assistance.

In bypassing state and local elected officials and funding programs directly through private organizations, the community action program created tensions and eventually prompted congressional action to restore the political control of local elected officials over antipoverty efforts. This shift was completed in 1981 when the Community Services Administration (which administered the funding of the local agencies) was dissolved and Congress incorporated its budget in a community services block grant (CSBG). The majority of the money from CSBG is allocated to community agencies formerly supported under community action, with a small amount of discretionary funds devoted to such programs as community economic development, rural housing, migrant farm workers, and youth projects. Despite reduced funding and pressure from the administration to eliminate CSBG entirely, the community agencies have persevered. Yet it would be a mistake to view the current activities of these agencies as fulfilling the promise of the community action philosophy of 1964, for in most communities they have neither the power, the resources, nor in some cases the will to mobilize and represent the poor. Nevertheless, the surviving community agencies have continued to convey the needs of the poor to less sensitive institutions while offering a broad range of services more consistent with traditional approaches to federal antipoverty programs.

Closely related to the community agencies is Volunteers in Service to America (VISTA), also established by the 1964 antipoverty law to enlist volunteers for the antipoverty effort. Although VISTA merged with other volunteer efforts (such as retired senior volunteer program, foster grandparents, and senior companions) to form the ACTION program in 1971, a large percentage of the agency volunteers remain active on community projects. Their work varies, ranging from legal aid to community development to disaster relief. During the late 1970s, VISTA was forced to weather attacks on community action activities and attempts to dismantle the parent ACTION agency. The Reagan administration sought to phase out the VISTA program entirely, and indeed succeeded in slashing federal outlays for VISTA by 60 percent. When combined with restrictions on activist community organizing efforts, these budget cuts have sharply curtailed VISTA's ability to promote lasting changes in low-income communities.

As the second primary vehicle of the community action initiative, the antipoverty legal services program became one of the most controversial antipoverty experiments. As the interface between the poor and the institutions that community action sought to change, the law was a natural starting point in attempts to intervene on behalf of the poor. Whether in landlord-tenant problems, wage garnishments for unpaid debts, excessive interest charges and shoddy workmanship by ghetto merchants, or conflicts with police and juvenile authorities, the poor are the most likely to confront the law and the least prepared to cope with it. Although traditional legal aid societies have long provided some services to the poor, the antipoverty program was the first federal effort to expand access to legal services to help the disadvantaged in coping with the legal system.

Most of the cases undertaken by legal services projects involved fairly routine matters. More than one-third of the cases dealt with family disputes, such as divorce, nonsupport, and custody of children; three in ten dealt with consumer or housing problems; and one in ten was a noncriminal adult or juvenile proceeding. Of the remaining cases, two of every three concerned administrative disputes or decisions by government agencies that affected the poor. Although few in number, these cases attracted the greatest public attention and controversy because they challenged the operations of the political and legal system. Legal services may have made its most lasting mark in this advocacy role. Among the most far-reaching cases eventually decided by the Supreme Court were those that opened the public assistance rolls to more needy persons.

In its brief but stormy history, the legal services program in the Office of Economic Opportunity made friends among the poor and disenfranchised but also made many enemies within established power bases. As the effort to dismantle OEO reached its peak in 1973, several years of harsh criticism focusing on the legal services program culminated in the transfer of legal aid efforts to an independent Legal Services Corporation. The 1974 legislation creating the corporation included a wide range of restrictions on the agency and its attorneys, including bans on representation in cases concerning school desegregation, nontherapeutic abortions, and certain criminal cases. Later amendments to the Legal Services Corporation Act lifted a variety of other restrictions originally passed in 1974, including bans on political activity (partisan or otherwise), representation of juveniles, and the use of corporation funds for research, training, and technical assistance related to the delivery of legal services. The vast majority of cases now handled by the Legal Services Corporation are similar in nature to those confronted in the legal services program of OEO, but some of the freedom and autonomy to pursue legal issues of importance to the poor have undoubtedly been lost.

The third vehicle for community action adopted by the Great Society policymakers experimented with a radical approach to solving some of the fundamental, chronic problems that contributed to poverty. The vision of the community development corporations (CDCs) was to support a variety of community-based enterprises that included manufacturing firms, service ventures, retail establishments, and construction firms as well as diverse social programs. Having failed to create a self-sustaining economic base in poor communities, the Nixon administration shifted away from a reliance on CDCs in the early 1970s and chose alternative mechanisms such as the Minority Enterprise Small Business Investment Company (MESBIC) and the targeting of loans through the Small Business Administration. The Reagan administration favored the establishment of enterprise zones to achieve the same ends. In retrospect, there is little reason to believe that the enterprise zones, if approved by Congress, would fare any better than earlier efforts. To the extent that the benefits of the CDCs were not limited to the narrow realm of economic development, the shift in emphasis to economic development in isolation falls short of the community action role envisioned in the original CDC program.

Contrary to popular impressions, some community action programs have survived the onslaughts on them and are reasonably well, albeit in modified form compared to the hopes envisioned for them by the Great Society antipoverty warriors. The most aggressive elements of the community action concept are gone, frequently co-opted by the very institutions and power structures they were designed to challenge on behalf of the poor. Yet there remains a strong and active strain of community participation and of greater awareness of the needs of the poor, as the community agencies continue to attempt to organize the poor and to provide a wide range of essential services on their behalf.

The Overlap of Cash and In-Kind Aid

The overlap of cash and in-kind assistance is inevitable, and, in many cases, desirable. For example, virtually all public assistance recipients receive medical benefits, 80 percent get food stamps, and almost one in four live in subsidized housing. Some families on public assistance receive none of this in-kind assistance, while others may benefit from several programs. About 6 out of 7 OASDI recipients are helped by medicare.

The most obvious—and intended—result of this overlap is an increase in the economic well-being of recipients. Some proponents of in-kind assistance hope that the qualified needy will benefit from as many programs as possible. But there are very serious problems not only in coordinating eligibility for these benefits but in adjusting the level of these benefits as outside earnings change. The present arrangement of administering most of these programs separately exacerbates this problem.

The disincentives to work have a devastating effect on AFDC families, who are the ones most likely to be able to supplement their assistance with earnings and are also most likely to benefit from one or more in-kind programs. As an AFDC family's earnings rise, its members are confronted with a decrease in their assistance payment (losing 67 cents in aid for each dollar earned after the first $30 and work expenses), a social security tax of 7.05 percent on all covered earnings, and federal income tax if their earnings exceed $8,400 for a family of four. In net cash income alone, an AFDC family receives limited rewards for working.

Table 4. Benefits potentially available to a female-headed family of four, 1984

Earnings	AFDC[1]	Taxes		Earned income tax credit	Net cash	Food stamps[2]	Net cash and food stamps	Medicaid[3]
		Social security	Income					
$ —	$4,416	$ —	$ —	$ —	$4,416	$2,185	$6,601	$2,050
1,000	4,416	67	—	100	5,449	1,939	7,388	2,050
2,000	3,676	134	—	200	5,742	1,915	7,657	2,050
3,000	2,676	201	—	300	5,775	1,969	7,744	2,050
4,000	1,676	268	—	400	5,808	2,023	7,831	2,050
5,000	676	335	—	500	5,841	2,077	7,918	2,050
6,000	—	402	—	500	6,098	2,034	8,132	—
7,000	—	469	—	375	6,906	1,788	8,694	—
8,000	—	536	—	250	7,714	1,542	9,256	—
9,000	—	603	312	125	8,210	1,296	9,506	—
10,000	—	670	442	—	8,888	1,050	9,938	—

[1]Assumes the state pays $368 per month and a standard $40 disregard and work expenses of $75 a month.

[2]Assumes a $95 standard deduction and an 18 percent work expense deduction on total earned income.

[3]Based on Census Bureau estimate of 1983 market values for medicaid excluding institutional expenditures.

If the family also receives food stamps, the incentives to work are further diminished. In addition, a most perverse problem arises from medicaid. The program covers all of a beneficiary's medical expenses or none. When a family is no longer eligible, all benefits cease. A family of four that receives the average benefit of $2,050 each year may lose all of this assistance by earning an extra $100. Families who also receive school lunches and public housing are confronted with an even more difficult choice.

The cumulative decrease in benefits as income rises—the cumulative tax rate—is illustrated in table 4. Maintaining meaningful work incentives for a family receiving several forms of aid is one of the thorniest problems in welfare reform.

Given the multiplicity of income-support and in-kind programs and the diversity of eligibility rules and certification procedures, there is room for persons to exploit the system. No doubt some have. A tendency exists, however, to exaggerate the inequities resulting from duplication. For example, a General Accounting Office study found that participation in multiple programs was largely a function of family size—large families face multiple needs and tend, therefore, to participate in more programs. It is doubtful whether a single cash assistance program could provide for all these needs.

Additional Readings

Fuchs, Victor R. *How We Live: An Economic Perspective From Birth To Death.* Cambridge: Harvard University Press, 1983.

Joe, Tom. *Profiles of Families in Poverty: Effects of the FY1983 Budget Proposals on the Poor.* Washington, D.C.: Center for the Study of Social Policy, February 1982.

Kahn, Alfred J. and Kamerman, Sheila B. *Social Services in International Perspective: The Emergence of the Sixth System.* Department of Health, Education, and Welfare. Washington, D.C.: U.S. Government Printing Office, 1977.

Levitan, Sar A. *The Great Society's Poor Law.* Baltimore, Md.: Johns Hopkins University Press, 1969.

Lewis, Charles E.; Fein, Rashi; and Mechanic, David. *A Right to Health.* New York: John Wiley & Sons, 1976.

U.S. Bureau of the Census. *Estimates of Poverty Including the Value of Noncash Benefits: 1983,* Technical Paper No. 52. Washington, D.C.: U.S. Government Printing Office, August 1984.

U.S. Bureau of the Census. *Quarterly Economic Characteristics of Households in the United States.* Current Population Reports, Series P-70. Washington, D.C.: U.S. Government Printing Office.

U.S. Congress, House Subcommittee on Health and the Environment of the Committee on Energy and Commerce. *Indian Health Care: An Overview of the Federal Government's Role.* Washington, D.C.: U.S. Government Printing Office, 1984.

U.S. Congressional Budget Office. *Federal Subsidies for Public Housing: Issues and Options.* Washington, D.C.: U.S. Government Printing Office, June 1983.

U.S. Department of Agriculture. *Food Stamp Program.* Washington, D.C.: U.S. Government Printing Office, July 1984.

Discussion Questions

1. "It is undesirable to provide poor families with food, housing, medical care, and other 'in-kind' payments at cut-rate prices. When subsidies are desirable, the government should provide cash subsidies and allow people to spend it as they wish." Discuss.
2. Some have argued that in order to estimate the number of poor people, it is necessary to include the value of in-kind income they receive. What are the technical difficulties in costing out in-kind goods and services?
3. Why has in-kind aid to the poor grown more rapidly than cash assistance over the past twenty years?

4. Consider the factors that have contributed to the rapid cost increases in providing health care for the poor.
5. What have been the criticisms of public housing programs that provide shelter for the poor?
6. How do the goals of community action agencies differ from the objectives of providing social services for the poor?
7. A significant phenomenon of recent years has been the increasing overlap between the wage structure and the benefits available from public assistance programs. What are the reasons for this development? What do you see as the consequences? Appraise the political prospects and potential effectiveness of proposals designed to deal with this phenomenon.

4. Programs for the Next Generation

Train up a child in the way he should go; and when he is old,
he will not depart from it.   —Proverbs 22:6

The experience of the past two decades—especially the ever-increasing costs of programs and services for the poor—offers some sobering lessons for federal policy. Under the Great Society of the 1960s, antipoverty programs were advocated with an optimistic view of the potential of federal efforts in aid of the poor, believing that a major commitment could eradicate poverty in our lifetime. The events of the 1970s suggested that it is a much more difficult and expensive endeavor. Not only have the poor remained, but the cutbacks in funding during the 1980s have shown the nation's growing reluctance to provide the level of support necessary to meet even the most basic needs of Americans below the poverty level.

There is no question that the immediate needs of the poor—income, food, shelter, health care—continue to place the most pressing demands on government funds for the poor. Yet the costs of these efforts are a constant reminder of the importance of steps to reduce the ranks of the poor in the future. Funds for the prevention of poverty may not show definite, positive results for many years, but they are still the cornerstone of help in an affluent society.

The obvious focus of prevention efforts is the next generation, the children of the poor. The federal role in attempting to shield the next generation from poverty has centered on three major areas: birth control, child care, and education. Assisting couples in keeping family size within their desires and means will aid the next generation to begin at less of a disadvantage. Providing care to preschool children can alleviate the pressures of poverty that bring the neglect of physical and social development during crucial formative years. Investing in the education of the next generation will better equip the children of the poor to compete in the job market and to find alternatives to dependency.

The heavy reliance on the direct provision of services to the next generation—as opposed to additional cash assistance to the poor for these purposes—is hardly accidental. In some cases, the in-kind approach is the only way to ensure effective aid; for example, cash assistance to defray the costs of birth control information or devices would probably not increase their availability or use by the poor. Direct provision of other services, such as education, is warranted because of economies of scale and the abiding interest in a universal system of education.

Birth Control

The close relationship between large families, unwanted births, and poverty is well documented. As the number of youngsters in a household increases, so does the probability that the family will be destitute (see figure 3). Unfortunately, data support the adage that "the rich get richer and the poor get children." Contrary to the widely held notion that the poor have more children because they want them, a longitudinal survey of about 5,000 American families conducted by the University of Michigan's Survey Research Center indicates that economic status and race have little bearing on the desired family size. All wanted approximately the same number of children, but lower-income families were less successful in maintaining their desired family size and the additional mouths to feed either pushed the near-poor into poverty or aggravated the plight of the poor.

Over the years, family planning has become increasingly prevalent and the quality of birth control methods has improved. In addition to scientific and technological advances, these gains reflect changing laws and societal values associated with birth control. The most significant legal change was embodied in the 1973 Supreme Court decision that struck down restrictive state laws regarding abortion, particularly during the first three months of pregnancy. Yet shifts in public attitudes toward abortion and birth control have played an equally important role in the extension of family planning. In 1968 about seven of eight adults opposed abortion when the desire not to have another child provided its sole justification. Less than five of eight Americans held this view in 1984. Back in 1959, 73 percent of adult Americans surveyed believed that birth control information should be available to anyone who wants it. Today the availability of birth control information is hardly considered an issue, even among Catholics.

Notwithstanding changes in bedroom technology and law, as well as the greater availability and acceptance of birth control, unwanted and unplanned births are still significant factors in

American society. The incidence of unwanted births remains greater for the lower-income and poorly educated population. The University of Michigan survey found that destitute families have about a one-third chance of an unwanted baby. For households earning about twice the poverty level or more, this probability falls to under 25 percent. A woman with a college degree has only about an 8 percent chance that she will have an unwanted birth, but for women who have less than a high school diploma the likelihood of unwanted births rises to roughly 33 percent. Limited access to birth control devices and family planning services clearly has prevented many low-income women from exercising the same degree of choice as their more affluent counterparts.

The continued importance of family planning efforts is illustrated in the rising frequency of births to unwed mothers. In 1982 almost one of every five births in the United States was without the blessing of church and state. The percentage of all children born out of wedlock has grown dramatically, nearly tripling over the last few decades. More than half of all black births and about one of every fourteen white births are out of wedlock. The highest concentration of out-of-wedlock births is among teenage women, who are the mothers of 40 percent of all children born out of wedlock. Women under 20 give birth to about 600,000 children per year; of this total, nearly one-half are out-of-wedlock births. In almost nine of ten cases, the teenage mother decides to keep the child; 8 percent are put up for adoption while the rest are sent to live with other relatives. Black teenage mothers on average show a higher propensity to keep out-of-wedlock children than white teenagers.

There is ample evidence that a teenage single mother is going to face diverse difficulties in rearing her offspring with lasting effects on both mother and child. The mother's education is likely to be interrupted as her child restricts her ability to acquire a basic education and secure a job. Studies show families headed by young mothers are seven times as likely to be in poverty as other families, and therefore are more likely to end up on welfare. More than half of the budget for AFDC is spent on families begun when the mother was a teenager. Even if the parents do marry and support their offspring, their education is still likely to be interrupted and their job opportunities may be limited for life. There is also considerable evidence that early parenthood leads to larger families, placing continuing economic burdens on the household and society.

The interrelated problems of teenage pregnancy and out-of-wedlock births pose one of the most troubling and challenging problems for public policies in aid of the poor. As in the past, unwanted births to teenage unwed mothers continue to stem in part from the poor's limited resources and access to family planning services, including information and birth control. Yet it is also clear that complex social and psychological forces have contributed to the rise in out-of-wedlock births and subsequent increases in the number of female-headed, single-parent households. Lack of meaningful life options for many impoverished young women appears to render motherhood an attractive alternative, providing a defined role as well as a sense of purpose and achievement. While the causes leading to the increasing propensity of low-income women to choose to have children out of wedlock may be poorly understood, this growth in female-headed households clearly portends greater poverty and dependency in the years ahead.

In recognition of the relationships between family size, out-of-wedlock births, and poverty, the federal government has played an active role in family planning over the last two decades, and in more recent years has devoted special attention to the prevention of adolescent pregnancy. Prior to the 1960s, family planning services were generally available only through private physicians and clinics. As part of the social security amendments of 1967, however, the Child Health Act required that family planning services be made available to AFDC recipients and special project grants were provided for such services. Legislation passed in 1970 established an office of population affairs in the U.S. Department of Health, Education and Welfare and authorized funds for family planning services, training, information and education programs, and population research. The program helps fund more than 5,000 of the country's family planning clinics.

It is estimated that nearly 7 million poor and near-poor women are annually in need of organized family planning services. The cost of providing a patient with a medical examination and birth control devices is about $82 a year. A comprehensive program to furnish services would cost about $560 million annually. Although total funding for family planning services has risen dramatically over the last two decades, the allocation of resources to this area remains considerably below anticipated need. In 1982 the federal government spent $275 million on family planning services compared to only $16 million in 1968 (excluding payment for services provided by private physicians). This federal support is channeled through a variety of programs: Title X of the Social Security Act ($118 million), medicaid ($94 million), social services block grants ($46 million), and maternal and child health block grants ($17 million). In addition, outlays for population and contraception research have increased from $8.4 million to $92 million since 1968. Data on family planning outlays by state and local governments and private organizations are not available.

As a result of increasing federal expenditures in support of family planning, the number of women served by federally funded programs rose from under 1 million in 1968 to more than 4.5 million thirteen years later (figure 13). Roughly six of every seven clients had low or near-poverty incomes. An additional 1.6 million low-income women received family planning services from private physicians. The nation's progress in this area is undeniable. Nonetheless, about a third of eligible low-income women of child-bearing age received no subsidized family planning services in 1983.

Since 1978, the federal government has also supported special efforts to reduce the incidence of teenage pregnancy. In response to increasing out-of-wedlock births among teenagers, Congress resisted Reagan administration efforts to include the adolescent pregnancy program in its block grants to states for maternal and child health, instead retaining the separate categorical program for this purpose. However, revisions adopted in 1981 did stipulate that one-third of federal outlays for the adolescent pregnancy program be used for research, with the remaining two-thirds provided for family planning and prevention services (including the counseling of teenagers to discourage premarital sexual activity). Federal outlays for programs related to adolescent pregnancy totaled $13.5 million in 1984, and individual states could use additional federal funds provided under maternal and child health block grants for this purpose.

The early 1980s have brought controversial changes in federal policies regarding family planning. Despite increasing public acceptance of birth control and a stated goal of reducing future welfare costs, the Reagan administration's approach to federal support for family planning services has ranged from seeking to reduce federal family planning expenditures to turning over responsibility for such programs to the states. Furthermore, federal funding of abortions through medicaid since 1981 has been limited to those few cases in which abortions are necessary to save the life of the mother. By failing to provide greater assistance to the poor so that they can achieve their desired family size and reduce out-of-wedlock births, the Reagan administration has undermined its own efforts to lower future welfare expenditures and promote self-sufficiency among the least fortunate.

Figure 13. Number of patients receiving family planning services

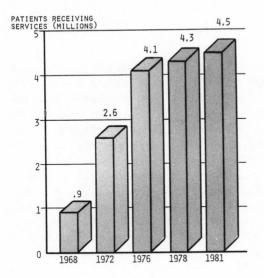

Source: Alan Guttmacher Institute

Just as AFDC payments are only one of the many costs of poverty, lower welfare costs are only a part of the total savings that accrue from family planning programs. The major reason for providing assistance to prevent the birth of unplanned children is not dollar savings, but rather the reduction of human deprivation. Family planning services can substantially improve health among the poor. Having too many children too close together contributes significantly to infant mortality, mental retardation, physical defects, and premature births. Frequent pregnancy is recognized as a health hazard to the mother as well, draining her energy and contributing to high maternal death rates. The Department of Health and Human Services has confirmed that fertility control is the most effective means of reducing infant death rates and improving maternal and infant health, particularly among teenagers who are more likely to suffer from maternal and infant morbidity. There are ancillary health benefits associated with family planning efforts as well; for example, physical examinations for low-income women help in detecting cervical cancer and other diseases. Finally, the long-term payoff of fertility control lies in the fact that children in smaller families tend to receive better care and are less likely candidates for a life of poverty than children in larger families.

Child Care

The impact of poverty on children can be lasting, and its imprint of deprivation lies at the very root of intergenerational poverty. The home environment has a fundamental influence on the development of children, and the offspring of the poor often grow up without the benefit of many forms of support—emotional, social, intellectual, and financial—that would move them closer to the realization of their full potential.

Previous chapters have already touched upon some of the federal programs that address the most basic needs of poor children, including medical services and child nutrition efforts. With the proportion of preschool children whose mothers work or look for work rising along with the efforts to induce poor women with children to enter the work force, federal outlays for child care programs have grown rapidly since the Great Society focused on the special needs of poor children.

In the 1970s the federal government broadly embraced the concept of child care as a major public responsibility in meeting the needs of the next generation. The principal source of federal support for general child care services is the social services block grant administered by the Office of Child Development in the Department of Health and Human Services. A total of $2.7 billion has been appropriated for the block grant in 1985. Each state receives a share of this amount based upon its population. Under the block grant formula, states have broad discretion over which services to fund with this money, although virtually every state provides child day care services. In the past, over one-fifth of all federal social services outlays went to child care. Now that individual states can make their own funding determinations, there is no certainty that the proportion of money allocated to child care will remain at this level.

Federal involvement in child care also developed as a by-product of the creation of the work incentive (WIN) program, established in 1967 to place adult AFDC recipients in training programs and jobs as alternatives to welfare dependency. In order to enable AFDC mothers to participate in the program and to take on jobs, the legislation requires states to provide child care arrangements for women enrolled in the program. Both in-home arrangements and formal facilities involving large numbers of children must meet standards developed by the state. The federal government provides 90 percent of the financing. Day care or child development facilities can also be provided as a social service under AFDC. States may set up facilities in poor neighborhoods and provide day care to any child supported by AFDC.

The complete list of federal programs offering support for child care services encompasses a broad range of legislative initiatives, including the community development program administered by HUD, the community action agency programs funded by the community services block grant, the employment and training programs run by the Department of Labor, state child welfare programs assisted by the Department of Health and Human Services, and more limited efforts funded through the Appalachian Regional Commission and the Bureau of Indian Affairs.

The largest federal subsidies for child care are provided through indirect tax expenditures, including an estimated $1.7 billion in federal tax credits for child care expenses in 1984. In addition, working AFDC recipients can deduct a maximum of $160 per child per month for child care expenses. While less visible, these mechanisms for indirect support of child care have a dramatic impact on the ability of parents to afford appropriate day care and other child welfare services. These programs may also address themselves to the child's health and general development.

The rising outlays for child care in the 1970s were accompanied by a federal debate regarding the appropriate content of child care services and the need for federal standards governing the provision of such services. At worst, child care can be merely shuffling children from one destitute household to another while depriving them of the personal attention that they might receive from their own families. At best, it can offer opportunities for learning, socializing, and individual care by professional staff that surpass the potential of the home environment, although the cost of this type of comprehensive care runs high.

The concept of federal staffing requirements for day care services generated intense controversy during the 1970s. Stringent federal standards were developed as early as 1968 but proved impractical to enforce on federally supported child care projects because the requirements would have raised costs dramatically and would have reduced the ability of public and private agencies to serve low-income families. Under the provisions of the Omnibus Budget Reconciliation Act of 1981, these federal standards were dropped, requiring instead that day care centers meet only applicable standards of state and local law. With the number of children under six years of age who have mothers in the labor force reaching 8.5 million in 1982, these relaxed standards may give a larger segment of the working poor access to day care services. In light of the importance of early childhood development, however, the tradeoff between the quality and quantity of child care services will remain a difficult one in the years ahead.

Education

Institutions outside the home are playing an increasingly important role in socializing and educating children and adolescents. The home environment still has a fundamental influence on the young, and poverty can seriously and permanently impair their ability to exploit educational opportunities. Impoverished children often experience great difficulties during their school years, not only because of health deficiencies and inadequate diets but also because they lack verbal and sensory stimulation in their family environment. Older youths face difficulties in high school and may drop out of school because their motivation and resources are limited. Children from poor families must have special attention from the very start if they are to succeed in school.

Most local institutions are unable or unwilling to offer this assistance. In poor neighborhoods, where schools are typically deficient in resources, facilities, and personnel, the federal government has developed a variety of supportive services to help children from impoverished homes mature into independent adulthood. Such services range from assistance for preschool children to financial support for indigent youths in college.

In 1984 the federal government expended $14.4 billion for educational programs. Most of these programs were targeted at serving the poor, handicapped, and minorities, although direct federal assistance to college students was aimed at a much broader clientele, and major portions of the other programs frequently missed their target. Nonetheless, it is estimated that more than one-third of the federal education outlays did reach the poor (table 5).

Head Start

A major development in public education during recent years has been the recognition that children from poor homes need preschool programs to compensate for their background deficiencies and to bring them closer to the achievement and adjustment levels of their more affluent peers. The Head Start program was initiated under the 1964 Economic Opportunity Act to meet this need and is

Table 5. Estimated federal investment in education for the poor, fiscal 1984

	Total outlays	Estimated outlays for poor
	(Millions)	
Total	$14,425	$5,364
Elementary and secondary		
Early childhood	958	824
Elementary and secondary	3,368	1,718
Other	748	157
Higher education		
College preparatory programs	165	134
Student financial assistance	3,257	1,205
Student loan program	3,136	627
Work study	569	188
Other		
Vocational education	698	91
Adult education	92	58
Indian education	326	140
Handicapped	1,108	222

Source: *Budget of the United States, 1985*

presently authorized under the Head Start Act. Over the years it has become the largest public child care and development program. Focusing on four- and five-year-old children, the program served 430,000 children in 1984 at a total cost of $958 million.

Despite the growth of the Head Start program, the vast majority of children from low-income households remain without the benefit of compensatory preschool education. In 1984 Head Start managed to serve just over one-fourth of all eligible children, a proportion that has risen only slightly since the mid-1970s. Even among the two in seven poor children participating in the program, the majority attend for only part of the day. If all eligible children who could participate in Head Start were served in full-year programs, the price tag would be in excess of $4 billion, an indication of the overwhelming size of the challenge in attempting to reach a larger segment of poor children prior to their entrance into elementary schools.

Although congressional appropriations for the Head Start program have barely kept pace with inflation, the program has continued to offer unique, important educational support to poor children. Because Head Start pupils have serious deficiencies that require individual attention, the program has a lower than usual student-teacher ratio. Like other antipoverty efforts, the program has emphasized the employment of subprofessionals and volunteers to relieve the teacher's work load and provide additional attention to the child. Many of these workers are mothers of children participating in the program. Parental involvement is a major goal of the Head Start effort. A child's needs cannot be met without parental cooperation and it is hoped that beneficial changes in the home environment may be a spin-off effect of the program. Bringing parents into the day-to-day operation of the centers has proven an effective way to advise parents about childrearing practices and to increase their interest in their children's education.

The Head Start program has made a significant contribution, dramatizing the educational needs of the poor and offering a program package for dealing with the problems of children from low-income households. The program has helped disadvantaged children "catch up" with their peers and has challenged local school boards that may have lacked the understanding, concern, or commitment to cope with the special needs of children reared in poverty. Compensatory education efforts such as Head Start are expensive propositions, but they remain one of the soundest investments in the next generation.

Research conducted on the Head Start program has provided substantial evidence that Head Start positively influences nearly every aspect of childhood development. Longitudinal studies of Head Start indicate that by reducing the likelihood of later handicaps and repeated grades, the program actually leads to a net reduction of public expenditures. Furthermore, research has shown that 67 percent of Head Start children graduated from high school, compared with 49 percent of a control group without compensatory education; 38 percent enrolled in college or a postsecondary vocational school, compared with 21 percent of the others; and 59 percent found a self-supporting job, compared with only 32 percent of the control group. Head Start children were also less apt to be arrested (31 percent compared with 51 percent) or to seek welfare payments (18 percent compared with 32 percent). Based on these findings, the investigators estimated that taxpayers save nearly $5 in reduced crime, welfare, public education costs, and increased tax revenues for every $1 invested in preschool compensatory education programs (or $3,100 for each child in the program). The effectiveness of the Head Start approach has been partly responsible for the stability in its funding in a period of sweeping budget cuts.

It has been argued that the current educational system acts as a sorting device rather than an equalizing system. Education services are delivered more effectively to children of well-educated and affluent parents than to those of poor parents. Whether Head Start is successful depends ultimately on whether it can induce changes in the American public school system and lessen deleterious influences in home life. More than a shift of goals is necessary, for substantial funds are required for the program's continuation. It has been estimated that the cost of compensatory education runs twice as high as the education of children from affluent homes.

In an endeavor to provide continuity of effort, Congress authorized a Follow Through program in 1967 to extend Head Start services into the early years of primary school. Because the follow through program has never enjoyed the congressional support that has maintained Head Start appropriations in recent years, the exploration of extended education services has been limited to a series of pilot projects testing the effectiveness of differing educational strategies. The program was to be phased out entirely by 1984, but Congress has continued to appropriate funding for the project, with $22 million for fiscal 1985.

Elementary and Secondary Education

While the special education needs of children of the poor have shaped only one aspect of federal child care efforts during the preschool years, the commitment to equal educational opportunity for children from all economic backgrounds has provided the fundamental rationale for federal involvement in what is still perceived as a state and local responsibility. In particular, federal programs have responded to the needs of poor neighborhoods where elementary and secondary schools are typically deficient in resources, facilities, and personnel, and to the special financial and supportive needs of children from low-income households who wish to pursue higher education.

The Education Consolidation and Improvement Act (ECIA) of 1981, a revised version of the Elementary and Secondary Education Act of 1965, is the primary vehicle for federal aid to the disadvantaged within the nation's public schools. By far the most important initiative under ECIA is the Chapter 1 program for compensatory education, which offers aid to state and local programs for educationally disadvantaged students residing in school districts with high concentrations of children from low-income families. Although the great majority of Chapter 1 funds are distributed to local educational agencies to supplement programs for students in low-income areas, funds are also available for state-operated programs serving handicapped, migrant, neglected, and delinquent children. In 1984 Chapter 1 provided $3 billion to school districts enrolling large numbers of poor children. An additional $451 million was expended in grants to states to help children in state-operated institutions.

Unlike Head Start, which distributes funds to states according to an allotment formula based on prior expenditures, AFDC payments, and demographic data, Chapter 1 funds are distributed in a block grant to state educational authorities, who in turn reallocate the funds to local school districts. The average expenditure of $536 per child was utilized for additional education materials, teachers' aides, speech and reading specialists, and other services to assist almost five million children. The Chapter 1 funds are allocated mostly to primary schools, with an insignificant proportion going to secondary schools.

Given the immense magnitude of the Chapter 1 undertaking—representing nearly one-third of all federal support for education programs serving poor children—the question of its effectiveness has drawn unwavering interest since its inception. The program structure itself has generated some legitimate criticisms. Federal aid is primarily available to local educational agencies serving areas with relatively high concentrations of poor children. Most of it is allocated on the basis of the number of children aged 5 through 17 who are in poverty, in families receiving AFDC payments, or are neglected, delinquent, or foster children. Funds may also be used, however, to assist any student who is "educationally deprived," regardless of family income. Although the intent of avoiding segregation in schools based on family income is laudable, this provision has created grave obstacles to the effective monitoring of the use of Chapter 1 funds at the local level.

A Department of Education study of Chapter 1 showed that the compensatory education program serves more children who are not from poor families than it does low-income or AFDC children. This problem is more disturbing in that the program serves only an estimated one-third to one-half of all children who need compensatory instruction, and that many of those served do not receive the full range of services they might require. Even though funds have been used to help nonpoor children or have been misdirected for other purposes, ECIA has directed needed funds into districts where the poor concentrate and has opened possibilities for compensatory education.

With safeguards added over time to ensure appropriate use of federal funds for compensatory education, the Chapter 1 program has narrowed disparities in achievement between poor and nonpoor children. Evaluations of Chapter 1 conducted for the U.S. Department of Education found positive, although modest, long-term gains in achievement and educational attainment among low-income children. The program has demonstrated the greatest degree of success in improving reading capabilities during the early elementary grades and in strengthening arithmetic skills in all elementary grades. While Chapter 1 expenditures may have been too diluted in early years to produce measurable gains, this federal aid appears to have had a cumulative effect on the cognitive development and educational advancement of children from low-income households.

Postsecondary Education

Although its value in the marketplace may be diminishing, the sheepskin is still one of the surest avenues out of poverty. Yet, as in many other areas, poverty itself is the greatest barrier to participation in higher education. Only one-fourth of young people from families with annual incomes below $10,000 attend college, compared with over one-third from families with incomes between $10,000 and $20,000 and half of those from families with incomes above $20,000 per year (figure 14). These data indicate the extent to which insufficient money, motivational supports, and prior education combine to discourage the children of the poor from attending college. It was in response to these barriers to a college education that programs administered by the Department of Education, including Upward Bound and Special Services, were created.

The Upward Bound program seeks to motivate students early in their high school careers and to help set their sights on college. Institutions of higher education receive grants to offer summer training and remedial education, including residence on a college campus as well as tutoring throughout the school year. Most students enter after the tenth or eleventh grade and attend two or three summer sessions before entering college.

The target population for Upward Bound, like that of the other federally sponsored college prep programs, focused on first-generation college students (those whose parents do not have a college degree) and low-income students whose families have incomes below 150 percent of the poverty level. Unfortunately, Upward Bound has been able to serve only a small fraction of the students who might benefit from participating in the program. Under these circumstances, it is not surprising that administrators have chosen the most promising students for enrollment in Upward Bound.

These concerns notwithstanding, Upward Bound has produced

Figure 14. College enrollment by annual family income, 1982

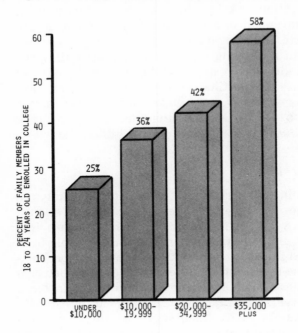

Source: U.S. Bureau of the Census

some encouraging results. Nearly six of every ten Upward Bound high school graduates have entered college. More importantly, at least 60 percent of those who enrolled in college were still in attendance two years later, indicating that Upward Bound students are as likely to remain in college as students from more affluent backgrounds. The effectiveness of Upward Bound also suggests that the program has selected students with maximum potential. If funds were available to help more young people from poor homes, the proportion entering college would undoubtedly drop.

There has also been an attempt to develop community-based programs that promote participation in college education. One such program focuses on the identification of poor youths with exceptional potential for college education, while another fulfills a similar role in providing adults with information on educational opportunities and supportive and financial assistance services. A related program providing special services for disadvantaged students is designed to assist students in meeting postsecondary academic standards. These projects often place between 75 and 90 percent of their students in postsecondary institutions. The House Committee on Education and Labor estimated that 20 percent of all college minority freshmen in 1982 were assisted by federally supported projects. Despite the inability of these programs to overcome large educational deficiencies from earlier years, they are effective mechanisms for bolstering student motivation and providing the extra support necessary to guide poor youths in postsecondary education.

In providing a comprehensive range of services that attempt to lower diverse barriers to college education, these preparatory programs are the most specifically targeted federal effort to assist youths from poor families to enter college. Yet in spite of the importance of these support services to educational opportunity, their impact would be minimal in the absence of the much broader and far more expensive commitment to student financial assistance. Federal programs offering grants, loans, and work to low- and middle-income students have grown rapidly in recent years, rising to a total of nearly $7 billion in 1984. Now reaching over 5 million students, federal student aid has dramatically reduced the financial barriers to opportunities in postsecondary education.

The greatest strides in financial aid have been made since 1972, when amendments to the Higher Education Act created the Basic Educational Opportunity Grant (BEOG) program. Authorizing a maximum award of $1,900 or one-half the cost of attendance (whichever is less), the basic grants have become the cornerstone of federal support for low-income students in postsecondary education. In 1984 over 2.6 million students received BEOG support (known as Pell grants), with an average grant award of $990; 70 percent of all recipients were from families with annual incomes below $12,000.

In addition to the BEOG program, Congress has established supplemental grant programs intended to assist students attending high-cost institutions and to encourage states to match federal funds for student financial aid. The program is administered by postsecondary institutions that receive allotments of federal funds based on student population and need. The program, which offers a maximum award of $2,000, assisted 655,000 students in 1984 with an outlay of $360 million.

The federal college work-study program offers another source of financial support to needy students, allowing participants to earn up to $200 in excess of demonstrated financial need, with the federal government covering up to 80 percent of the cost. Most institutions of higher education participate in the program, with students working up to 20 hours a week during the academic year and up to 40 hours a week in summer work programs. The rates of pay are set by the participating institutions, although the 1980 amendments to the Higher Education Act prohibited the payment of subminimum wages in programs. A total of $569 million in federal outlays was devoted to college work-study programs serving approximately 870,000 students in 1984.

To supplement direct financial assistance, the national direct student loan program extends long-term loans to low-income students at 5 percent annual interest. The guaranteed student loan program is not limited to serving the poor, but is part of an overall strategy set by Congress with the goal of meeting 75 percent of a student's cost of education through a combination of family contribution and grant aid. In 1984 the federal government spent over $3 billion on student loan programs.

Another federally supported education program is administered by the Veterans Administration. Since the end of World War II, the VA has offered financial support for veterans who wish to continue their education or training. Two separate educational benefit programs are available for veterans. For those who entered the military before January 1, 1977, monthly stipends—amounting in 1984 to $342 for single veterans and $407 for a veteran with one dependent—are available under the GI bill. Measured either by cumulative outlays or numbers of students served, the GI bill has been one of the most massive federal commitments to student financial assistance in higher education and has been recognized as a key vehicle for the advancement of young people from low income families. Persons who entered the military after that date are entitled to participate only in a contributory educational assistance program. Under this program, the veteran must have contributed between $25 and $100 a month, up to a maximum of $2,700 while in service, in order to be eligible. These funds are matched by the VA at a rate of $2 for every $1 contributed by the participant if they are used to obtain an education; otherwise they are returned to the veteran. The majority of veterans taking advantage of these benefits enroll in college, though enrollment in vocational, professional, business, or high school is also acceptable. The educationally disadvantaged and black veterans have failed to participate in the same proportions as whites and high school graduates. To encourage disadvantaged veterans to benefit from the programs, the law provides that time spent on remedial courses or tutoring to correct an educational deficiency can be added to the entitlement, with no reduction in the 36-month limit on benefits. By the end of

1983, over 900,000 veterans had participated in these "free entitlement" programs to overcome their educational handicaps.

Federal and state governments also continue to make major investments in institutional aid, and the lower student costs in state-supported colleges and universities in particular can be directly traced to this indirect approach to subsidized education.

In reviewing the comprehensive system of student financial aid now supported under federal education programs, it is tempting to assume that financial need is no longer a major barrier to participation in higher education in the United States. Even if we had reached this goal in the 1980s, however, it would be impossible to ignore the ominous forces that threaten to destroy the ability of the federal government to support this extensive financial aid system as the decade continues. With predictions of sharp declines in college enrollments during the 1980s, the temptation to cut federal aid may gather support. But with tuition hikes exceeding cost of living increases, demands for additional federal support of student aid are likely to mount. In addition, the adequacy of federal aid to poor youths is threatened by the gradual extension of student grants and loans to middle-income families. This combination of sharply rising educational costs and a political mandate for a broader distribution of student aid funds has the potential for undermining federal efforts to meet the financial needs of poor youths throughout the 1980s, and yet there is no doubt that the advances of the past two decades have gone a long way toward enabling aspiring youths from impoverished homes to complete a college education.

Child Welfare Services

Children's aid programs were the first social welfare services provided by the federal government, dating back to the Taft administration. While child and maternal services are not aimed exclusively at children of poor families, most beneficiaries are from low-income families. A government brochure describing child welfare services, for example, announces that they are designed "for troubled children and children in trouble." Problems of child neglect, abuse, and emotional disturbance are not found exclusively in indigent homes, but it is hardly surprising that poor children face more than their share of such problems. Consequently, children from impoverished homes are likely candidates for assistance offered by child welfare programs.

Federal programs to promote child welfare address a broad

range of problems, including child abuse, foster care, adoption, runaway youths, and research related to these problems. By far the largest federal child welfare expenditures go to support poor children in foster care. This assistance, formerly provided as part of the AFDC program, is now channeled through the states as an entitlement for all foster care children meeting AFDC eligibility criteria, with individual states determining the level of payments to foster parents or institutions. In addition to income support, foster care children receiving this federal assistance also become automatically eligible for medicaid benefits. Federal outlays for foster care totaled $440 million in 1984 and supported benefits to 98,000 children each month.

The states also receive federal grants for the provision of child protection, foster care, adoption, and other child welfare services to children and their families without regard to income. These discretionary funds are intended to encourage state-administered activities which promote family reunification, assist children considered to be at risk, and provide adoption or foster care alternatives when necessary. Federal funds are distributed to the states on the basis of the population below age 21 and per capita income, and small additional grants are made available to support training activities for child welfare workers or students and teaching grants for related curriculum development. Total federal expenditures for child welfare services and training reached $169 million in 1984.

Other federal initiatives to promote child welfare operate on a much smaller scale, with combined outlays for several categorical programs barely exceeding $50 million in 1984. In response to growing concern over child abuse, the federal government provides block grants to states in support of prevention and treatment efforts, funds research and demonstration projects related to such activities, and sponsors projects to facilitate and encourage the adoption of children with special needs. A separate federal program supports runaway shelters and services such as counseling and referral for youths under age 18 who run away from home. Finally, the federal government provides modest support for ongoing research and demonstration projects in the field of child welfare, including studies of the special needs of abused, disadvantaged, and foster care children.

When compared to the size and scope of federal expenditures for child care and education, the federal investment in child welfare services hardly looms large. In part, these limited outlays reflect a historic view of child protection and welfare as predominantly state responsibilities. Yet as public awareness of child abuse, neglect, or inadequate supervision and protection has increased, the impetus for federal involvement and encouragement of state activities has grown. For a small minority of children at risk, these federal programs ensure continued state efforts and research activities to address their pressing needs.

Additional Readings

Anderson, Bernard E. and Sawhill, Isabel V., eds. *Youth Employment and Public Policy.* Englewood Cliffs, N.J.: Prentice-Hall, Inc., 1980.

Butler, Erik and Mangum, Garth. *Applying the Lessons of Youth Programs.* Salt Lake City, Utah: Olympus Publishing Company, 1982.

Carnegie Council on Policy Studies in Higher Education. *Giving Youth a Better Chance.* San Francisco: Jossey-Bass Publishers, 1979.

Grant, W. Vance and Snyder, Thomas D. *Annual Digest of Education Statistics.* Washington, D.C.: U.S. Government Printing Office.

Levitan, Sar A. and Alderman, Karen Cleary. *Child Care and ABCs Too.* Baltimore, Md.: Johns Hopkins University Press, 1975.

Levitan, Sar A. and Belous, Richard S. *What's Happening to the American Family?* Baltimore, Md.: Johns Hopkins University Press, 1981.

Rossi, Robert J. *Summaries of Major Title I Evaluations.* Palo Alto, Cal.: American Institute for Research, 1977.

Discussion Questions

1. Evaluate critically the claim that free birth control services are the most cost-effective means to fight poverty.
2. Do you believe that child care is an effective tool to combat poverty?
3. Explain the rationale for compensatory education and college preparatory programs for disadvantaged youths.
4. Granted that a sheepskin is a passport out of poverty, should the federal government undertake the responsibility of subsidizing higher education?
5. Based on the experiences drawn from federal social welfare programs discussed in the preceding three chapters, discuss the strengths and weaknesses of cash transfers and in-kind aid in attacking social problems.
6. "The myriad of social welfare schemes to alleviate poverty is not only costly but is a disincentive to work. The only way to get people off of 'welfare rolls' and onto 'payrolls' is to work through the marketplace by offering businesses tax incentives to hire disadvantaged workers most in need." Comment.
7. What proposals, if any, would you offer for mitigating poverty in the United States and why?

5. Opportunities for the Working Poor

*Anticipate charity by preventing poverty; assist the reduced fellow
man . . . so that he may earn an honest livelihood, and not be forced
to the dreadful alternative of holding out his hand for charity. This is
the highest step and the summit of charity's golden ladder.*

—Moses ben Maimon

The goal of the antipoverty programs as stated in the preamble of
the Economic Opportunity Act of 1964 is "to eliminate the paradox
of poverty in the midst of plenty in this Nation by opening to
everyone the opportunity to live in decency and dignity." In order
to carry out this goal, more is needed than direct cash payments
and the provision of goods and services that might lessen the
burden of poverty but fail to attack the causes of dependency.
Programs that provide opportunities for self-support and permanent exits from poverty are crucial to its elimination in the long
run. As an old proverb moralizes, "Give a man a fish and you feed
him for a day. Teach him to catch a fish and you feed him for life."

Those in need of self-help programs are found in a variety of
situations. Some of the unemployed lack the skills to compete
effectively in the labor market, and others are qualified workers
unable to locate a demand for their skill. There are also some, not
counted among the unemployed, who are too discouraged by their
failure to find work to continue to look. In addition, there are
employed persons counted among the "working poor." They are
part-time workers who need full-time work to keep them out of
poverty and persons employed at such low wages that even full-
time work does not raise them above the poverty standard. These
underemployed and low earners, when added to the unemployed
and discouraged, constitute the subemployed. The subemploy-
ment rate gives a more realistic indication of the universe of need
for employment and training services.

The range of self-help programs for the employable poor is wide.
Some programs focus on the supply side of the labor market,
preparing the poor for gainful employment. These include most of
the employment and training programs launched in the 1960s and
1970s. Other programs are directed to the demand side, opening
doors for the poor in private labor markets and in past years even
providing public employment for those not absorbed in the private

sector. A third group of programs seeks to improve the functioning of the labor market for the poor, matching up supply and demand more effectively and setting standards and minimums for low-income employment. Finally, several programs deal with all three of these aspects of the labor market, but concentrate on a specific geographical area or population group.

Employment and Training

To help the structurally unemployed and to induce the poor to enter the labor market, the federal government has sponsored a number of employment and training programs responding to their various employment needs. Although not all the programs are specifically targeted at the poor, poverty households are the prime beneficiaries of many of the services offered. These efforts have been sharply reduced by the Reagan administration, but they still provide a wide variety of labor market services and carry a substantial price tag—amounting in 1984 to over $6.9 billion (figure 15). They include efforts directed to specific categories of clients and they offer in varying combinations the following labor market services:

1. outreach to identify the untrained and undermotivated as well as intake and assessment to evaluate their needs and abilities;
2. adult basic education to remedy the absence or obsolescence of earlier schooling;
3. prevocational orientation to expose those of limited experience to alternative occupational choices;
4. residential facilities for those who live in sparsely populated areas or who live in a debilitating environment that would adversely affect attempts to overcome their disadvantages;
5. work experience for those unaccustomed to the discipline of the work place;
6. job development and subsidized private employment;
7. job placement and labor market information services; and
8. supportive services—such as medical aid and child care centers for mothers with small children—for those who need assistance to facilitate entry into the labor market or resumption of work.

Few programs, if any, offer all the listed services, but there is a continuing effort to coordinate complementary programs. Often, however, participants do not receive the precise package they need and may be ineligible or unaware of needed programs. Nevertheless, evidence suggests that those who are served can benefit substantially from the programs.

Figure 15. Federal outlays for employment and training programs by type of service

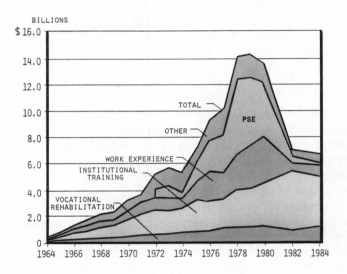

Source: Budget of the United States Government, Fiscal 1985

The majority of the participants in the programs receive assistance in finding jobs, although frequently the jobs are only temporary. The estimated distribution of participants in federally funded employment and training services (excluding vocational education) follows.

	(Thousands)
Total	*5,769*
Skill training	835
Work experience	780
Job placement	3,030
Vocational rehabilitation	954

The poor often lack adequate knowledge of the labor market and the contacts needed to secure jobs related to their skills. Job development, information on available opportunities, instruction in job search technique, and referral service to employers increase their likelihood of finding employment. Basic education, vocational training, counseling, and work experience help make the poor more attractive to potential employers. Current employment and training programs can be divided into three major categories according to the services provided: those that emphasize education and training (including remediation), those that stress work experience, and those that focus on matching job seekers with appropriate employment opportunities. Some of the programs are aimed at specific population segments and provide overlapping services in attempting to meet program goals.

Skill Training

Vocational education is the oldest federal investment in job-related training, dating back to the Smith-Hughes Act of 1917. In 1984 federal expenditures for vocational education totaled about $698 million, with state and local governments contributing about $10 for each federal dollar. Most of the federal share was for matching grants to states for basic vocational education programs; the rest supported grants to states for consumer and homemaking education, work-study, cooperative education, vocational research, and other specific activities. Most of the federal money is distributed in grants to state governments, which then parcel out the funds to local school districts. State and local officials traditionally have had wide latitude in spending these funds, until a 1968 amendment began targeting federal dollars. Subsequent vocational education amendments have further increased federal discretion in determining how the grant money is to be spent. In the amendments of 1984, a new "set aside" provision earmarked funds for eliminating sex stereotyping in vocational education, serving prison inmates, and for training adults, including single parents and homemakers. Congress also required that 22 percent of the state grant be spent for disadvantaged students, including those with limited proficiency in English, and another 10 percent for handicapped students. Despite the attempt to direct more aid to the underprivileged, most school systems have tended to define disadvantaged broadly and have included many students who do not come from poor families. Inadequate records are kept by the states about students and program characteristics. Furthermore, some states have not been careful to restrict these funds to the designated students. Thus, help for the poor probably has not yet matched congressional intent.

Because students from poor families are considerably more likely to enroll in vocational curricula and are less likely to continue their education beyond high school, it is important that vocational courses qualifying them for jobs be available to them. Although enrollments have been shifting toward more salable skills, many students attend schools that offer few choices and quite a few are enrolled in courses that may offer little job-related training. It is important that vocational education keep pace with the rapidly changing job market in order to provide useful skills.

Many vocational education enrollees are adults and most are not poor. The educational needs of poor adults are more directly addressed by the $92 million adult education program designated for persons 16 years and older who lack a high school education. Because 29 percent of the heads of poor families who are 25 years old and over have completed only eight years of school or less and an additional 23 percent have less than a high school education, it is apparent that the poor form a large proportion of the more than 2 million enrollees in adult education courses. A number of the enrollees go on to job training programs, and many others benefit directly from their educational improvements by higher income.

The initial focus of skill training programs in the 1960s was to retrain workers whose skills had become obsolete as a result of changing technology. The Manpower Development and Training Act (MDTA) of 1962 provided institutional training for the unemployed and underemployed. In time, however, it became apparent that workers at the margin of the labor force, including a growing number of new entrants with little or no job skills, were even more in need of training. The institutional programs were expanded to include basic education, training allowances were increased in both amount and duration, and skills centers were established in some 80 communities to provide institutional training in a variety of occupations along with supportive services. Follow-up studies show that enrollees benefited from their training experience. They experienced less unemployment than control groups, and their earnings increased. The antipoverty efforts of the 1960s spawned a wide variety of programs as new problems were recognized, and by the early 1970s there was a clear need to consolidate and coordinate the diverse efforts. The Comprehensive Employment and Training Act (CETA) of 1973 was enacted to ease federal restrictions on program structure and to vest greater planning and implementing authority in state and local governments. The resulting federal-state-local partnership allowed increased flexibility at the local level to develop employment and training services to respond to local labor market needs. The CETA programs provided essentially the same basic services offered under the MDTA programs, allowing local program administrators to determine the service mix needed and how it was to be provided.

During the 1970s job creation in the public sector was a major component of employment and training programs, reaching a peak of 750,000 enrollees in 1978. As part of the Omnibus Budget Reconciliation Act of 1981, however, the program was eliminated. No other major job creation program has since been enacted to take its place.

The emphasis of training shifted again with the passage of the Job Training Partnership Act (JTPA), which replaced CETA in October 1983. The JTPA puts greater reliance on private sector placement, low training costs, and local autonomy. The new act also reduces federal funding for employment and training and curtails federal responsibilities for monitoring the use of such funds. In addition, stipends are no longer available for participants undergoing training, making it more difficult for poor persons who are not on welfare to avail themselves of the training programs. The effects of these changes on training will most likely hurt the poor, who are most in need of employment programs. The private sector, which is to have a controlling role on the training programs, will inevitably place greater reliance on work performance, thereby making it more difficult for the poor, who are typically unskilled and in greater need of job support, to receive training. It appears, therefore, that the JTPA has significantly altered the direction of employment and training programs away from helping the more disadvantaged workers.

Job Corps

A major concern of the training programs has been the employment of young people. The Job Corps, established by the Economic Opportunity Act of 1964, provides intensive and expensive vocational training and basic education to youths from 14 to 21 years of age who are poor, out of school, and out of work. Largely a residential program, it rests on the assumption that the most seriously disadvantaged young people must be removed from their debilitating home environments before they can be rehabilitated. Almost all Job Corps enrollees are from poor families, and most suffer educational deficiencies serious enough to sentence them to a life of poverty. Many have failed in other training programs or in finding and retaining jobs.

All enrollees receive basic education through teaching techniques especially developed for the illiterate and deficiently educated. On the average, they benefit more from this training than they did from their public schools, with educational achievement approaching public school norms. Vocational training of differing complexity is provided, and the corpsmembers receive a wide variety of supportive services, including room, board, health care, recreation, and a monthly allowance ranging from $40 to $100 depending on how long the participant has been in the program. There is also a readjustment allowance for those who stay in the Job Corps to provide a financial cushion for them upon leaving the program. Advanced career training was added during the late 1970s to the options available to corpsmembers showing exceptional motivation and achievement. The total cost of these services is high—$15,250 per corpsmember year, or in excess of $7,500 per enrollee in 1984—but largely unavoidable if residential training is to be provided to unemployed, out-of-school youth.

Benefit-cost studies reveal that the investment in the Job Corps program does pay off. In 1984, the Job Corps served approximately 80,000 youths in about 107 centers with a capacity of 40,000 slots. Among the 41,500 terminees who were available for placement in fiscal 1981, 35,800 were either placed in jobs, entered school or the military, or engaged in further training. This is a significant achievement after an average of seven months of training when it is considered that the bulk of participants were from impoverished homes, more than 80 percent did not complete high school, and less than half had above a sixth-grade reading level at enrollment.

Work Experience

Even though federal job creation programs have been eliminated, two programs still exist that provide work experience for the nation's youth and part-time work for the elderly. The summer youth employment program, funded under the JTPA, allocates grants to states to subsidize minimum-wage, public-sector summer jobs for youths between the ages of 14 and 21. About 718,000 summer jobs were available under the program in 1984, giving poor youths an opportunity to gain early entry into the labor market.

At the other end of the age spectrum, the older Americans employment program provides part-time public service employment for older workers to help them retain their attachment to the work force. This program, which is authorized under Title V of the Older Americans Act, creates jobs contracts with public and private nonprofit national service organizations. Subsidized jobs of between 20 and 25 hours per week are provided for low-income persons 55 years of age and over. Outlays of $319 million in 1984 financed about 62,000 such subsidized jobs.

Employment Service

Besides the shortage of jobs and lack of skills, the employable poor also face obstacles in the labor market because they are unaware of existing employment opportunities and of training programs. The labor market frequently fails to match jobs with workers, and its inefficiencies are most noticeable in serving poor people.

The largest single delivery system of labor market services is the United States Employment Service (USES), established by the Wagner-Peyser Act of 1933. The system's 1,900 local offices placed 3 million individuals in various jobs in 1982, including a significant number of poor persons, primarily because the "work test" requires employable applicants for food stamp, welfare, and unemployment insurance to register for work at the USES. Though federally financed, the USES is administered separately in each state. As a result, services to the poor may vary significantly from state to state and from local office to local office.

The antipoverty efforts of the mid-1960s shifted the emphasis and responsibilities of the public employment offices toward aid for the poor. The volume of USES activity declined, largely because of this shift in emphasis away from serving employers and toward efforts to help the disadvantaged. In the 1970s, the service attempted to reorient its relations with employers and to secure more job vacancy listings by reaching out to nondisadvantaged applicants who could fill more of the available job opportunities and by advertising the benefits of this free job service to employers to secure more listings. An effort was made to improve job matching by computerizing data processing. But as a result of the work test registration requirements, the unemployed and the poor continued to constitute the bulk of the public employment service clientele.

As the public employment service was attempting through more efficient management to regain its former position in the labor market, the 1973 enactment of CETA created a new obstacle. The employment service had been the presumptive deliverer of outreach, counseling, placement, and other services prior to 1973. But state and local officials funded under CETA had the option of using other organizations to provide these services. The employment service accordingly lost some support, especially in urban areas. Despite the conflict that grew between the two agencies, accommodations and attempts to coordinate overlapping efforts emerged by the close of the 1970s.

The JTPA included amendments to the Wagner-Peyser Act to coordinate the employment service more closely with the JTPA's new training system. A new state allocation formula for employment service funding amounting to $890 million in 1984 bases distribution on labor-market needs. Greater responsibility now resides in the states in planning, oversight, and substate allocation functions. In an effort to give increased emphasis to the labor-exchange mission, those services unrelated to the basic function of the employment service are performed on a cost-reimbursable basis.

Work Incentive Program

The goal of the work incentive program (WIN) is to induce welfare recipients to achieve economic independence and to stem the growth of welfare. Experience has shown the difficulty of achieving these goals. Enacted as a 1967 amendment to the Social Security Act, WIN was to provide comprehensive services leading enrollees to economic independence. Because enrollees often needed basic education and skill training as well as child care and other supportive services, success was modest and costs were high. Indeed, even many who had successfully completed the program did not earn enough to leave the welfare rolls.

In reaction to such limited results, the Talmadge amendments, which took effect in 1973, increased federal matching to make the program more attractive to states and deemphasized classroom training in favor of direct job placement. In the succeeding years, the proportion of funds spent on skill training dropped steadily, while the proportion spent on job placement rose, transforming WIN into a delivery agency rather than a training organization. In fiscal 1982, over 1 million persons were referred for registration and development of employability plans, and an estimated 203,900 persons obtained unsubsidized employment. Only one-fourth of those who found employment, at an average hourly rate of $4.35, were placed in jobs directly by WIN.

The Reagan administration proposed doing away with the WIN program, substituting reliance on workfare—mandatory job search and other employment related activities for AFDC recipients—in its place. Rather than granting specific budget appropriations, the administration proposed that states use social services block grant or JTPA funds to provide welfare recipients with employment and training services. Congress rejected Reagan's proposal, however, and has allotted $270 million for administration of the program in fiscal 1985.

Vocational Rehabilitation

Job training as well as medical, educational, and other needed services are offered to the physically and mentally handicapped under the federally supported vocational rehabilitation programs. The 1965 legislation included poverty as a disabling handicap,

reasoning that the case-by-case approach of vocational rehabilitation, which provides a variety of services according to
individual needs, would prove an effective means of preparing
disadvantaged people for satisfactory employment. While few
persons are selected on the basis of poverty alone, many of the
disabled are poor.

The vocational rehabilitation program has played a significant
role in preventing poverty. During 1984 there were 954,000 active
cases and the agency claimed that 220,000 persons were rehabilitated. One can only speculate whether the reported success
rate of the vocational rehabilitation program would be achieved if
it were extended to more of the severely disabled with low incomes
or to poor persons in general, but the existing program is effectively
enhancing the employability of a large number of physically and
mentally handicapped poor people, and it is preventing others
from becoming economically dependent.

Equal Employment Opportunity

Job discrimination has been a major cause of poverty among blacks,
Hispanics, families headed by females, and other minority groups.
Recognizing that some among the poor have been denied jobs or
advancement solely because of their sex, race, or national origin,
Title VII of the 1964 Civil Rights Act bans discriminatory hiring
and employment practices.

The five-member Equal Employment Opportunity Commission
(EEOC), created to implement Title VII, is empowered to bring
lawsuits against respondents charged with violating the law. In the
first fifteen years following the formation of the EEOC, the courts
broadened the definition of discrimination and clarified the pa-
rameters of unlawful employment practices. In 1979 the Supreme
Court held that race-conscious affirmative action plans were permitted where designed to overcome de facto racial imbalances in
an employer's workforce. Until then, all employment preferences
based on race were uniformly regarded as illegal.

The Supreme Court had previously ruled that practices that
were fair in form, but resulted in the disparate exclusion of minorities or women, violated the statute. Specifically, it outlawed pre-
employment tests that were not job-related, permitting only those
selection devices or procedures that fairly predicted a job applicant's performance.

Though the EEOC has never been granted power to issue cease-
and-desist orders against employers, it steadily expanded its en-

forcement activities during its first 15 years. Of particular significance was the adoption in 1978 of the enforcement strategy focusing on "systems of discrimination." Under this approach, employment practices resulting in empirically measurable underutilization of minorities or women were held to constitute a violation and were subject to legal action by the agency. Class action suits on behalf of groups of employees produced multi-million dollar consent decree agreements in the late 1970s with American Telephone and Telegraph Company, General Electric Company, and other major firms.

The federal government has also urged compliance with nondiscrimination in employment practices by using its substantial market leverage. Before the Reagan administration the Office of Federal Contract Compliance Programs (OFCCP) required all firms providing goods or services to the government to establish affirmative action goals and timetables. The OFCCP originally focused on construction, aiming to increase the hiring of minority craft workers by contractors. Minority employment at union wage levels has increased in most crafts, although employment in proportion to minority availability in most local area labor markets has not yet been reached.

Under the Reagan administration, efforts to combat employment discrimination have been narrowed to include only the most flagrant violations. The administration has rejected the use of quotas, numerical goals, and timetables as a means of correcting for past discrimination, and required that an intent to discriminate be demonstrated before remedial action be taken. Based on its commitment to reduce federal regulation and intervention in private sector practices, the Reagan approach to civil rights and equal opportunity has relied heavily on voluntary compliance. The administration has shunned active measures to promote equal employment opportunity, preferring to review only those specific complaints lodged by aggrieved individuals and civil rights organizations.

This narrow interpretation of federal responsibilities has been reflected in the Reagan administration's outlays and enforcement proceedings to promote equal employment opportunity. Real outlays for civil rights and equal opportunity enforcement throughout the federal government declined by 9 percent from fiscal 1981 to fiscal 1983. After adjusting for inflation, the EEOC budget was reduced by 10 percent and the OFCCP budget slashed by 24 percent during the same three-year period. These budget cuts have been coupled with cumulative staff reductions of 12 percent in EEOC and 34 percent in OFCC between 1981 and 1983. Finally, despite an increasing number of complaints during this period, the number of employment discrimination cases initiated by the EEOC and the Department of Justice dropped to only half of what it had been.

Minimum Wages

The persistence of poverty among the working poor testifies to the maldistribution of societal rewards for work and the need for improvement. A job—even full-time employment—is not a sure escape from poverty. In 1984 a worker would have had to earn $5.10 an hour (assuming that the employee worked at least 2,000 hours annually) to lift a family of four out of poverty. However, over 10 million adults were employed at or below the minimum wage, which stood at $3.35 an hour in 1984, the same rate it has been since 1981.

Though most of these low-paying jobs are filled on a part-time basis by secondary earners or by youths, there is also a significant number of family heads who work regularly but are unable to escape poverty. In 1983 almost 1.3 million poor family heads held down a full-time, full-year job. There were also 382,000 unrelated individuals working full time, full year, but remaining in poverty (figure 16).

The plight of these adult working poor receives little attention in training and employment programs already described. These programs tend to be preoccupied with the unemployed, youths, and those outside the labor force. The goal of most training programs is full-time employment; that this may be no real solution to poverty is often ignored, as are the needs of those who are already laboring at full-time, low-paying jobs.

The minimum wage is perhaps the most direct and comprehensive measure to increase the earnings of the working poor. The objective of the Fair Labor Standards Act (FLSA) of 1938 was to achieve, as rapidly as practicable, minimum wage levels that would sustain the health, efficiency, and general well-being of all workers. An unduly high or rapidly rising minimum might price many low-productivity jobs out of existence, so that the gains from higher wages have to be balanced against the losses from job elimination.

On the assumption that a low-paying job is better than no job at all, Congress has acted incrementally in applying the law over the years. It has established minimum wages that directly affect only a limited number of employees at the bottom of the economic ladder. About four of five nonsupervisory workers are covered by the

Figure 16. Work experience of the poor, 1983

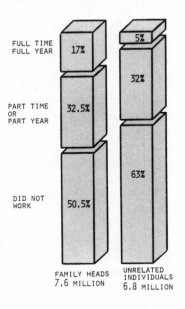

FULL TIME
FULL YEAR 17%

PART TIME
OR
PART YEAR 32.5%

DID NOT
WORK 50.5%

5%

32%

63%

FAMILY HEADS
7.6 MILLION

UNRELATED
INDIVIDUALS
6.8 MILLION

Source: U.S. Bureau of the Census

minimum wage. Still not covered are 9 million private-sector nonsupervisory employees, many of them in low-wage occupations, primarily in retail trade, outside sales, service industries, and agriculture. A 1976 Supreme Court decision removed many state and local workers from federal FLSA protection. Though state minimum wage laws provide some protection to excluded workers, these standards range widely and are usually below the federal minimum wage.

One can only speculate about the number of workers whose earnings are boosted by the minimum wage, but some insights can be gained from reviewing the incremental increases in the minimum wage and extensions in coverage. It was estimated that the 1977 law initially boosted the wages of 4.5 million workers, which gives an indication that wages tend to cluster around the minimum wage for millions of employees.

The favorable impact of minimum wage rates is reduced to the extent that employers find it unprofitable to retain or hire workers at the government-imposed wage levels, resulting in job loss or reduced work rather than higher earnings. Because many factors are involved, it is difficult to determine the extent of job elimination resulting from the federal law. The available evidence indicates that the minimum wage legislation has raised the total income of the poor, and that any losses in employment and earnings were more than compensated by the increased earnings of the majority. This is, of course, little comfort to individuals who lost their jobs as a result of such increases. Nor do studies of changes affecting those now employed tell the whole story. Future demand for labor might be dampened, closing off potential job opportunities for those who might otherwise have been hired.

Arguing that the youth unemployment problem is largely the result of minimum wages, the Reagan administration favored a lower minimum wage for teenagers, claiming that more jobs would be created at lower wages. The assertion remains unproven. Even had there been no minimum wage, youth unemployment would still have been a serious problem. Moreover, if more jobs became available for youths, there is no guarantee that the gains would not be at the expense of displacing adult workers. However, true to the adage that there is no free lunch, the minimum wage does entail some costs. Accordingly, support has developed for a youth minimum wage which would permit a lower minimum for all youths under 18 during the summer months. Despite strong backing by the Reagan administration, such a proposal has not yet been enacted.

It is questionable, however, whether a reduced youth minimum wage would have a significant impact on youth unemployment. The major causes of unemployment among black teenagers and other disadvantaged groups must be sought elsewhere. First, the liberalization and expansion of various income support measures, including AFDC, have offered a minimal measure of income maintenance to young women with children. Some may have preferred to subsist on relief rather than to work at very low wages. Second, some black unemployment reflects suburban housing discrimination. Jobs once open to blacks in central cities disappeared with the exodus of middle-class white and black families. As jobs moved to suburbia, many residents of slum areas became economically stranded owing to inadequate public transportation or the lack of private "wheels." Third, demographic factors and an increased supply of black youths in central cities must also have contributed to increased unemployment, particularly since, as already suggested, the demand for their labor declined.

To minimize the dangers of unemployment and inflationary pressures, proponents concede that minimum wages should be raised no more rapidly than average wages in American industry. While little is known about productivity trends in low-wage industries, it is reasonable to assume that the rise in productivity in these industries is no greater than in the rest of the American economy. If this assertion is correct, a rule of thumb might be that boosts in the minimum wage should be no larger than rises in the cost of living, plus average productivity increases.

In an inflationary economy it may be desirable to raise the minimum rate periodically to keep pace with the rising cost of living, at least more often than Congress is likely to enact new legislation. One way both to adjust the minimum wage to increasing living costs and to avoid the discontinuities of infrequent but large jumps is to index the minimum to a cost-of-living measure, in line with automatic adjustments made in social security and other benefits. In 1977 Congress rejected a proposal to index minimum wages, providing instead for four annual raises boosting the minimum hourly rate to $3.35 by 1981.

Some advocates have argued for setting minimum wage rates high enough to eliminate poverty among all full-time workers. Regrettably, such pronouncements are more rhetoric than serious policy alternatives. Reasonable people may differ on whether the current minimum wage should be extended to additional millions of workers or whether it should be adjusted to a predetermined proportion—say, 50 percent—of average wages in American industry. There can be little doubt, however, that excessively rapid boosts in the minimum wage would cause serious economic dislocations and loss of jobs. It would be a case of killing the goose that lays the egg, even if the minimum wage would buy little gold. Eliminating jobs is not the way to fight poverty.

Without diminishing the past achievements of the minimum wage, it would be unrealistic to place excessive reliance upon such legislation as a tool to combat poverty. Policymakers must consider the trade-off between boosting the minimum wage as a means of reducing poverty and the danger of eliminating jobs as a result of such actions. In the final analysis, conclusions regarding the impact of minimum wage legislation upon aggregate employment and unemployment depend on value judgments, and whatever the conclusion some relevant facts can be found to support the views. If society is determined to reduce poverty at a more rapid rate than in the past, reliance upon additional tools will be necessary.

Migrant Workers and Undocumented Aliens

As a group, migrant workers are a seriously deprived segment of the work force. Most are blacks and Mexican-Americans based in southern Texas, California, and Florida. Almost half of all migrant workers have less than a high-school education, and one of seven has completed less than five years of schooling. They usually live in substandard housing, both at their base residences and while traveling. Dilapidated housing, low incomes, and lack of protection from employment-related injury and illness foster poor health conditions. These workers follow the harvest as far north as Minnesota, Washington, and New York each year, often paying farm labor contractors to find them jobs at wages bringing an average annual income considerably below the poverty level.

Because they are on the move from spring until fall each year, migrant workers are difficult to reach through the standard federal social and welfare programs. Residency requirements and difficulties in certifying their incomes limit their access to such programs as medicaid, food stamps, welfare, and job training. Given their meager incomes, child labor becomes a necessity, in defiance of laws designed to keep the children in school.

Employment prospects for migrant workers are declining steadily as more mechanical devices are introduced in the harvesting process. There has been no significant increase in rural nonfarm employment to absorb displaced workers. Moreover, these working poor are not entitled to the protection of federal labor laws providing for unemployment compensation and collective bargaining or of many states' workers' compensation laws. Therefore, the need to train migrant workers and to provide basic education to their children is pressing if the poverty of these families is not to be visited on future generations.

Even the serious problems of migrant laborers are probably not as severe as those of illegal immigrants. Foreign nationals who enter or work in the United States in violation of U.S. immigration laws are typically subjected to oppressive working conditions and low wages. Yet, because these undocumented workers are deportable aliens, they have few remedies to enable them to protect their constitutional rights, and little access to public aid or support.

Although many of these illegal immigrants come from the Caribbean, Asia, Africa, and Europe to find unauthorized employment in major metropolitan areas throughout the United States, the majority illegally cross the 2000-mile United States–Mexico border, often with the help of smugglers. Like virtually all other illegal immigrants, Mexican undocumented workers are at the same time pulled into the United States by the lure of higher wages and pushed out of their native land by very low standards of living and the lack of employment opportunity.

U.S. policy since the turn of this century has alternately discouraged, encouraged, and ignored the entry of illegal Mexican labor, depending on the health of the U.S. economy and its demand for cheap labor. In recent years, however, the number and ethnic diversity of illegal immigrants entering the United States appear to have increased substantially. In recognition of the greater need for control over the influx of illegal immigrants, the enforcement resources of the Immigration and Naturalization Service have correspondingly increased as well. INS apprehensions of illegal immigrants have increased more than tenfold over the last two decades, from approximately 110,000 per year in 1965 to about 1.2 million annually by 1983. Despite the significant rise in the number of apprehensions, however, there are still estimated to be between 4 and 7.5 million illegal immigrants residing in the United States today.

Like our immigrants of the past, the undocumented alien of today tends to be a young, unskilled adult male, in search of economic opportunity on a scale that he cannot find in his home country. Though the data on this clandestine population are scanty, and despite the fact that the majority have had little schooling and speak no English, the jobs that they obtain are not just menial or low-wage. Surveys of apprehended illegals have estimated the proportion employed in farm work at only about one-fifth, with substantial numbers finding work in manufacturing, construction, and services. This wide range of jobs means that some workers obtain relatively good wages. According to one source, the average hourly wage for these illegal immigrants was one-third higher than the minimum wage but one of ten earned less than the minimum wage.

Large numbers of illegal aliens in the labor force and their penetration of a broad range of industries and occupations present a policy dilemma during periods of high national unemployment. Legal and illegal immigrants and refugees contributed half of the country's net labor force growth during the early 1980s, meaning that many of them are holding jobs that could be filled by some of the nation's unemployed. Because illegals are often willing to work hard under adverse conditions for low wages, they tend to depress wage rates, slow improvements in working conditions, and hamper unionization efforts in agricultural and manufacturing industries, particularly in the southwestern states where they have clustered until the 1970s. Consequently, illegal immigrants are most likely to adversely affect low-wage, mainly minority workers in the United States, forcing some individuals who would otherwise have jobs to depend on government support.

There is, however, the other side of the argument over illegal immigrants. Defendents of these undocumented workers claim that the estimates of illegal immigration are exaggerated. Moreover, they argue that immigrants do not displace workers or depress wages because they typically fill jobs that U.S. citizens are unwilling to take. Finally, there is the claim that immigrants pay more in taxes and payroll deductions than they withdraw in social services.

The debate over illegal immigration has led to difficulties in adopting an acceptable immigration policy. A bill recently debated in Congress proposed a number of sanctions to curb the flow of illegal immigration. The bill would have provided for increased enforcement funds for the INS, penalties for employers who knowingly hire illegal immigrants, exclusion and deportation of illegals, and an expansion of the temporary foreign worker program that would allow immigrants to work in the U.S. for a limited duration. The controversial nature of regulating immigration has continued to forestall action on legislation. Whatever measures are eventually adopted, the difficulties of controlling illegal immigration will remain as long as American borders are relatively open and there are economic incentives for poor Mexicans and those of other nationalities to seek higher-wage U.S. jobs.

Economic Development Programs

For a myriad of reasons rooted in regional economic trends and often in unique local conditions, poverty tends to become concentrated in specific geographic locations. Declining employment opportunities, high rates of out-migration, low per capita income, underdeveloped infrastructure, low educational attainment of the population, and a high percentage of farm employment interact in some localities to produce labor surplus or "depressed areas." The areas themselves vary. Poverty pockets exist in otherwise prosperous metropolitan areas, in underdeveloped rural areas, and in isolated or stagnating regions cut off from the rest of the economy. Some are as small as an inner-city neighborhood and others as large as Indian reservations or major sections of the rural South or Appalachia. The problems faced by rural and urban areas differ but are related. The out-migration plaguing many rural areas has resulted in an influx of unskilled migrants into the cities, whose middle and upper classes in turn have fled to the suburbs, creating poverty ghettos in the inner cities. Depressed urban and rural areas fail to attract new economic enterprise because they frequently lack adequate public facilities and the labor force tends to be deficiently educated and poorly trained.

While the history of federal efforts to promote area redevelopment can be traced to the New Deal programs of the 1930s, the major federal economic development programs emerged in the 1960s and received increased emphasis under the Carter administration in the late 1970s. The central thrusts of the economic development effort are directed by the Department of Housing and Urban Development, although the Departments of Interior, Agriculture, and Commerce, and the Appalachian Regional Commission also administer significant programs. Federal outlays in 1984 to aid labor surplus areas were distributed as follows:

	(Millions)
Total	$7,217
Community Development Block Grants (HUD)	3,900
Urban Development Action Grants (HUD)	480
Economic Development Administration (Commerce)	336
Rural Development (Agriculture)	1,134
Appalachian Regional Commission (Agriculture)	217
Bureau of Indian Affairs (Interior)	1,150

The Department of Housing and Urban Development has evolved into the major source of federal aid to depressed areas. HUD funds for community development are distributed in block grants to state and local governments for supporting a variety of urban renewal and community improvement and development activities as well as initiatives aimed at improving housing for the poor and stabilizing the community in general. With growing emphasis on federal block grants and local decisionmaking, communities are expected to integrate community development projects with employment projects under JTPA.

Congress considered problems of severely distressed urban areas in the Housing and Community Development Act of 1974 and later amendments that authorized urban development action grants (UDAC). A major focus of the UDAC program is to use public funds to encourage private investment in redevelopment projects in poverty areas. In 1984, $480 million was allocated through block grants to designated cities, towns, and urban counties to assist in revitalizing their economic bases and reclaiming blighted neighborhoods for renovation.

The Public Works and Economic Development Act of 1965, administered by the Economic Development Administration (EDA) of the Department of Commerce, provides grants for public works and other redevelopment projects, industrial development loans, loan guarantees and interest subsidies, technical assistance, and research and development grants. The future of EDA is uncertain, however, as the Reagan administration has proposed that it be phased out and its remaining functions transferred to other agencies.

While both EDA and HUD programs focus primarily on urban areas, the Department of Agriculture provides extensive aid to economically depressed rural areas and smaller communities. Authorized by the Rural Development Act of 1972, the Farmers Home Administration administers a major business and industrial loan program channeling, in 1984, $700 million in direct loan program guarantees to business and local governments in communities with populations below 50,000. The Rural Electrification Administration has served as the source of capital investment assistance to rural areas since 1936, financing subsidized loans for improved electrical generation and consumer services, and for the improvement and expansion of rural telephone service.

The Appalachian Regional Commission (ARC) represents a unique federal approach to economic development. Created under the Appalachian Regional Development Act of 1965, the commission is authorized to provide a broad range of federal assistance within a 13-state area extending from New York to Mississippi. Reflecting the underlying assumption of the legislation that the economic distress of the Appalachian region is due in large part to its relative isolation (and possibly because the several states involved could initially agree on relatively few concrete projects), the majority of the more than $3 billion Congress has appropriated over the years (through 1984) for the ARC has been allocated for the construction of a major highway system and additional access roads. The remainder of the funds are currently used to increase the federal share in grant programs, to finance health and child-development projects, to create vocational education facilities, to restore land ravaged by mining, and for other public facilities. How long such programs will continue to be funded is questionable, however, as the Reagan administration has proposed to terminate the ARC and its nonhighway access roads programs and continue only the highway system through funding from the Department of Transportation.

Quite obviously, jobs are created by the ARC's direct expenditures; but the long-term effect of improved transportation and infrastructure in attracting industry to the region is not clear. While federal aid to underdeveloped areas may offer significant boosts to local economies, it remains virtually impossible to separate the impact of federal policies from the constant fluctuations of business cycles and regional growth trends. In itself, federal economic development assistance is rarely provided in the massive or concentrated doses necessary to reverse the economic decline of truly distressed areas.

If the role of federal aid in economic development is uncertain, the effectiveness of programs for distressed areas in fighting poverty is even less clear. The federal policies toward distressed areas rely on a "trickle down" approach, concentrating on aid to the business community and assuming that such efforts will eventually generate new jobs that will help the unemployed in the future. While the attempt to provide incentives for businesses to locate or to expand enterprises in high unemployment and poverty areas may be justifiable on other grounds, it is necessarily a long-range strategy with little immediate antipoverty impact. Economic development programs will seldom offer direct relief to the poor, but they may help to minimize disparities in regional growth, thereby lessening the high concentrations of low-income households that compound difficulties in alleviating poverty.

Indian Programs

Federal programs for American Indians are a special application of the area approach to poverty. These programs provide a wide range of goods and services as well as income and employment for Indians living on or near reservations. This unusual concentration of federal support is a response to the serious deprivation that exists among the 486,460 Indians who live on 278 federal and state reservations and other trustlands, as well as a belated recognition of the government's culpability for the adverse conditions under which Indians live.

The highest incidence of concentrated poverty in the United States is found on Indian reservations. Comparative indicators emphasize this impoverishment. Indian families have an average income two-fifths as large as the average American family. This lower income must be shared by families that include twice as many children under 18 as the national average. Unemployment rates on reservations are several times higher than the national average, and a majority of reservation families live in unsanitary, dilapidated housing. Moreover, the violent crime rate on reservations far exceeds that for rural America; Indian schoolchildren drop out before completing high school at a rate double the national average; and the average life span of an Indian is signifi-

cantly shorter than the national norm. Obviously, reservation
Indians desperately need a federal program that employs an area
approach to their concentration of poverty.

Because of Indians' unique historical status as wards of the state,
the federal government has assumed broader responsibilities for
reservation residents than for other citizens. Altogether, the federal
government expended over $2.5 billion on programs for Native
Americans in 1983, mostly benefiting those living on or near
reservations. Besides the $834 million spent by various federal
agencies for social welfare and capital improvement projects on
reservations, the Indian Health Service and the Bureau of Indian
Affairs spent $1.7 billion on their programs (figure 17). While the
nearly $5,169 annual aid per individual Indian living on or near a
reservation may appear to be large on the surface, it must be noted
that the sources of additional funds for these Indians are very
limited. Lacking significant private resources or economic activity,
Indians on reservations must depend upon federal support for
essential services and goods.

Despite the relatively high per capita federal expenditures, the
"big brother" approach to solving reservation problems has not
worked. The reasons are complex. They include a failure to consider the Indian's cultural heritage as well as disputes within
federal agencies and among the Indians themselves regarding

Figure 17. Federal assistance to Indians, 1983

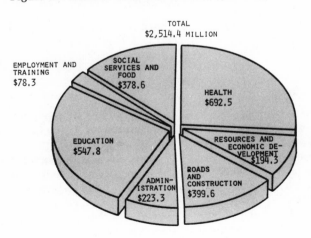

TOTAL
$2,514.4 MILLION

EMPLOYMENT AND TRAINING $78.3

SOCIAL SERVICES AND FOOD $378.6

HEALTH $692.5

EDUCATION $547.8

RESOURCES AND ECONOMIC DEVELOPMENT $194.3

ROADS AND CONSTRUCTION $399.6

ADMINISTRATION $223.3

Source: Office of Management and Budget

appropriate program goals. Paradoxically, if Native Americans are ever to free themselves from the federal government, even more federal aid will be necessary to develop their economic base and social institutions. Without this infrastructure, the Indian communities will be unable to contribute support to their own institutions.

Additional Readings

Anderson, Martin. *Welfare: The Political Economy of Welfare Reform in the United States.* Stanford, Cal.: Hoover Institution Press, 1978.

Blaustein, Arthur I., ed. *The American Promise: Equal Justice and Economic Opportunity.* New Brunswick, N.J.: Transaction Books, 1982.

Briggs, Vernon. *Immigration Policy and the American Labor Force.* Baltimore, Md.: Johns Hopkins University Press, 1984.

Levitan, Sar A. and Belous, Richard S. *More Than Subsistence: Minimum Wages for the Working Poor.* Baltimore, Md.: Johns Hopkins University Press, 1979.

Levitan, Sar A. and Johnston, William B. *Indian Giving.* Baltimore, Md.: Johns Hopkins University Press, 1975.

Levitan, Sar A.; Mangum, Garth L.; and Marshall, Ray. *Human Resources and Labor Markets.* New York: Harper and Row, 1980.

Levitan, Sar A. and Taggart, Robert. *Jobs for the Disabled.* Baltimore, Md.: Johns Hopkins University Press, 1977.

Levitan, Sar A. and Zickler, Joyce. *Too Little But Not Too Late: Federal Aid to Lagging Areas.* Lexington, Mass.: D.C. Heath and Lexington Books, 1976.

U.S. Bureau of the Census. *American Indian Areas and Alaskan Native Villages: 1980.* Supplemental Report. Washington, D.C.: U.S. Government Printing Office, August 1984.

U.S. Department of Labor. *Annual Employment and Training Report of the Secretary of Labor.* Washington, D.C.: U.S. Government Printing Office.

Discussion Questions

1. Summarize the salient facts concerning the impact of welfare upon incentives to work and sketch your favorite scheme for reducing conflicts between work and welfare.
2. In what ways can education and training be considered as investment?
3. What role does civil rights legislation play in combating poverty? Has the recent deemphasis on civil rights had any effect on poverty rates in the past few years?
4. Reconcile the claims that minimum wage laws eliminate jobs and that they protect the poor by raising their standard of living.
5. What were the economic and social forces, both long and short run, that led to the emergence of employment and training policies and

programs during the 1960s and 1970s? And what effect will the retrenchment of the last three years have on the effectiveness of employment and training programs?

6. "Rehabilitation, not relief," has been an implicit and explicit credo in U.S. antipoverty efforts. It is largely this emphasis that has so intertwined employment and antipoverty efforts. To what extent are employment and training policies and programs useful as antipoverty tools?

7. Do you believe that the government should consider company hiring and promotion practices in awarding contracts?

8. Discuss the concept of area depression and the problems associated with measuring this phenomenon. In what way are they the same? In what way are they different? What implications do these similarities and differences have for public policy? What public policies are presumably on the books to assist these less developed areas? Are they successful?

9. Analyze the conflict between the goals of Indian self-determination and their status under various treaties with the federal government.

10. What policy should Congress adopt with respect to immigration?

6. Strategies to Combat Poverty

*The needy shall not always be forgotten; the hope of the poor shall
not perish for ever.*   —Psalms 9:18

America took great strides during the 1960s to combat poverty. The
Great Society's antipoverty legislation launched a comprehensive
effort to meet the needs of the poor in our nation's history. While
the rhetoric of the war on poverty was muted in the 1970s, federal
social welfare expenditures continued to increase. The titles of
Great Society programs changed and their administrative structures
altered, but most antipoverty initiatives persisted nonetheless.

The Lessons of the Great Society

The Great Society efforts were rooted in a three-pronged strategy.
First, in an attempt to change the poor by bolstering their self-
sufficiency, the Great Society expanded education, training, and
other services. Second, to allow the poor a greater voice in determining their own destiny, the Great Society sought to increase their
access to American institutions and their participation in the
planning and implementation of antipoverty programs. Third, to
satisfy basic needs, the Great Society expanded direct assistance to
the poor through the provision of in-kind services, including
health care, shelter, and nutrition.

This combination of programs and services was designed to
provide a base of support for the current poverty population while
at the same time building a ladder out of poverty for the next
generation. The strategy was sound, but it also proved expensive.
Federal outlays rose moderately under the Johnson administration,
but the entitlements incorporated in the Great Society legislation
fueled accelerated budget growth during the first Nixon administration. By 1973, total federal outlays (after adjusting for inflation)
had more than doubled in the span of a single decade, leading to
concerns that the "budget explosion" was fueling inflationary
pressures. When the Nixon-Ford administrations moved to re-
strain the growth of the federal budget in the mid-1970s, few

136

doubted the need for such action. The fight centered primarily on whose ox was to be gored.

Without judging the merits of this shift toward fiscal restraint, it is evident that the Great Society's emphasis on opportunity and future advancement was sacrificed in attempts to halt the rapid expansion of federal outlays. The optimism of the Great Society was abandoned, replaced by a resignation embodied in the prophecy, "the poor ye shall always have with you." Federal support for education, employment, training, and related antipoverty programs that sought to enhance future self-sufficiency expanded, but not sufficiently to make serious dents in the institutional arrangements which could help combat poverty. By the late 1970s, investments in expanded opportunity had dwindled markedly in comparison to federal outlays for income support, and the failure to maintain a balance between these competing goals as envisioned in the Great Society assured that poverty would continue and even increase in the 1980s.

Several factors may have contributed to the nation's unwillingness to sustain the struggle against poverty as a top priority. The most flagrant deprivation in America had been alleviated by the 1970s, and yet the Great Society's hope for an easy and lasting victory over poverty had not been realized. Furthermore, the increasing reliance upon income transfers at the expense of programs to expand opportunity and self-sufficiency undermined political support for aid to the poor, reinforcing the image of government handouts without prospects for future advancement. Amidst the economic turmoil caused by deep recessions, accelerating inflation, and oil price hikes, national policymakers failed to commit the resources necessary for a sustained drive to eliminate poverty.

Thus, by the end of the 1970s, growth in aid to the poor had ceased. The plateau in federal aid to the poor under President Carter was transformed into a sweeping policy of retrenchment under President Reagan that was partially restrained by Congress. As a share of total federal expenditures, outlays for means-tested programs to aid the poor dropped from 21.5 percent of the budget in 1980 to 16.8 percent in 1983. The cumulative impact of this pattern of budget cuts is reflected in the Congressional Budget Office's estimate that households with annual incomes below $10,000 will lose more than $20 billion between 1982 and 1985 as a result of the Reagan administration's spending reductions.

The needs of the poor in the 1980s are no less pressing than they were two decades earlier. To the contrary, under the combined impact of rapid inflation, severe recessions, and reductions in federal social welfare expenditures, the number of the poor rose to 35.3 million in 1983, boosting the poverty count by 44 percent following the sharp drop during the preceding two decades. The national poverty rate increased from 11.4 percent in 1978 to 15.2 percent in 1983—the highest poverty rate since 1965. What has changed in recent years is the nation's readiness to place the goal of ameliorating economic deprivation at the top of the national agenda and to use the resources of the federal government to assist the poor. The first step in alleviating the plight of the poor therefore is necessarily a political one, requiring a reversal of the policies of retrenchment spawned by the Reagan administration.

The Great Society fell short of creating a simple or orderly program for improving the prospects of the poor. While millions of Americans living in poverty were given additional income through the expansion of public assistance, training stipends, and in-kind benefits, the nation failed to develop a universal system to meet the basic needs of the poor and to blend income support with services that expand future opportunity and self-sufficiency. The challenge in the years ahead lies in the development of an integrated approach to reducing poverty, one that provides greater hope for advancement and self-support while focusing federal resources on those areas and groups with the greatest potential or need. Only through greater reliance upon programs that offer the promise of opportunity as envisioned in the Great Society is the nation likely to reject policies of negativism and retrenchment for a more compassionate response to poverty in America.

A Comprehensive Program

A comprehensive program in aid of the poor should recognize that the poor need both income and services, not one or the other. It is essential to provide direct income support which meets basic needs, but a lasting response to the problems of the poor must emphasize those efforts that attack the causes of poverty rather than those that merely mitigate its symptoms. The two objectives are not easily separated, but the vast experimentation of the past two decades suggests some course of action for the next decade and beyond. Coupled with continuing research into the factors that contribute to its persistence, a commitment to use available resources to strike at the roots of poverty can yield significant progress.

Basic Support

It would be a grave mistake to overlook the advances made in the transfer system already in place. Although the several existing programs may seem disjointed and inefficient, in sum they form a fairly comprehensive, albeit not universal or uniform, system of income support. Each of the various programs has its own target group, but there are no longer major gaps in coverage, although some duplication is inevitable. The growth of the food stamp program and increased coverage under unemployment compensation have finally extended some aid to the working poor, while the federalization of adult public assistance categories has improved the lot of the disabled and aged poor who cannot work. These improvements in the current transfer system are significant, even if they do not obviate the need for additional resources to aid the poor.

Even assuming that a consensus can be reached on the amount of additional resources to be allocated for the attack on poverty, it is not obvious how these resources should be distributed and most effectively utilized. What share of any additional dollars should be allocated to raising the cash income of the poor and what share allocated to improving the quality and quantity of services that are offered to them? The poor are not a homogeneous mass. Additional income will provide for the basic needs of some; many others require services that will enable them to partake in the affluence of American society. Indeed, in view of the multiple problems faced by the poor, it is problematic whether a reasonable cash grant alone can provide for their basic needs.

Partly as a reaction to the expansion of services under the Great Society, the concept of a guaranteed income gained increasing popularity during the 1970s. This approach won support from both ends of the political spectrum: many liberals lauded the goal of a universal benefit floor providing greater equity and security for the poor, while some conservatives found a negative income tax or other income guarantee an attractive means of minimizing government intervention in the marketplace. In terms of the adequacy, simplicity, and efficiency of aid to the poor, the benefits of some minimal income guarantee for those in need have long been recognized. Yet the transition to a more direct income transfer system has proved difficult.

The classic dilemma for public policy lies in the balance between the minimum income guarantee, work incentives, and total program costs. A grant adequate to fulfill basic needs and an effective tax rate on benefits low enough to preserve work incentives combine to create a very expensive antipoverty program. For this reason, even the guaranteed income proposals advanced by the Nixon and Carter administrations failed to win the approval of Congress. For example, the Carter proposal would have established a minimum benefit level of 65 percent of the poverty level for AFDC recipients. Although considered a modest goal, it would have constituted a significant advance in building a base of federal support for the poor. Some critics believed that the proposals offered too little support to the destitute; others feared that a more generous level of guaranteed income would push program costs to unacceptable heights. The need to overhaul the current system of in-kind benefits and to accommodate state and local variations in benefit levels and in living costs also have stymied previous efforts to put a guaranteed income program in effect. Finally, the difficulties of spelling out operational distinctions between employable and unemployable individuals in the treatment of the poor remains a serious obstacle to preserving essential work incentives while also meeting the basic needs of those unable to work.

The plight of the working poor looms as one of the greatest barriers to the elimination of poverty. In the present transfer system, any attempt to raise the nonworking poor out of poverty would only create unacceptable work disincentives for the millions of Americans working and yet still living in poverty or just above the poverty threshold. The importance of channeling aid to the working poor in order to preserve work incentives received increasing recognition during the 1970s. The earned income tax credit passed in 1976 and subsequently expanded offers significant relief to the working poor through the tax structure, serving as a wage supplement that builds upon the modest security of minimum wage laws. Unfortunately, this progress in extending aid to the working poor has been halted and partially reversed by the Reagan administration in the early 1980s.

Under the rationale of targeting aid to the "truly needy," President Reagan's social welfare policies have actually reduced federal aid and work incentives for the working poor. Food stamp and AFDC budget cuts enacted in 1981 fell heavily upon those recipients with earned incomes, raising their marginal tax rates dramatically and forcing many off the welfare rolls. As a result of these changes, the disposable income of working AFDC families fell in every state in 1982, and in 12 states the impact on work incentives was so severe that a nonworking AFDC parent with two children ended up better off than a working parent in similar circumstances. Nationwide, the disposable income of the average AFDC working family dropped from $595 per month in fiscal 1981 to $476 in 1982, reducing their incomes from 101 percent to 81 percent of the poverty line. By cutting aid to working households and forcing them below the poverty threshold, the Reagan administration has left no room for an equitable program that could lift those who cannot work out of deprivation.

A more constructive and compassionate response to the problems of the working poor, as well as the nonworking poor who are employable, would be to broaden opportunities for advancement and self-sufficiency through work. In the short term, work incentives that would provide assistance to alleviate the hardship of the working poor and ensure that the rewards of work exceed the stipends of dependency should be restored. For the longer term, however, federal social welfare initiatives should focus on investments that enchance the ability of the poor to secure gainful employment and support their families with a decent wage. Although specific priorities are subject to debate, the following areas represent important places to begin.

Education

Over a century ago the people of the United States reached a consensus that free schooling should be made available to all. While publicly supported education expanded, little attention was given to lowering the entry age for poor children in publicly supported schools before the establishment of Head Start. The growing number of working women, including mothers with small children, now raises the need to expand preschool facilities on a universal basis. In light of the massive outlays required to establish needed facilities, school authorities might follow the practice adopted for school lunches, initially requiring more affluent parents to pay tuition to partially support such programs while children from poor families are admitted free. In any case, the expansion of child care and education services to preschool children, particularly those with working mothers, should be the nation's first priority: an investment in the next generation during its most formative and important years.

The other educational priority should be to target aid at the improvement of elementary and secondary schools, particularly in poverty areas. Remedial education is expensive and, to the extent that the additional investment would make the broader educational system more effective the first time around, federal aid targeted at poor communities can reduce the need for rehabilitative measures. The traditional mode of local school financing places areas of high poverty concentration at a severe disadvantage, and carefully monitored support for the improvement of local educational practice can restore some equity to educational opportunity in basic education. Remedial efforts will no doubt remain important to the poor, and the expansion of opportunities in post-secondary education offers a major escape route from poverty, but efforts in both these areas will prove futile without a sound base of preschool care and elementary and secondary education on which to build.

Employment and Training

Experience has shown that our economy may not generate an adequate number of jobs to employ the poorly educated and un-skilled. Creation of jobs for them should be second only to the establishment of adequate training facilities for those who are sufficiently motivated to acquire new skills. The continued high level of unemployment among the unskilled, particularly among blacks and other minorities, indicates the need to generate govern-ment-supported employment—not make-work jobs—for those who cannot qualify for gainful employment in private industry.

Despite the gloomy forebodings of the prophets of cybernation, much of society's needed work is not being done, and the needs are going to increase rather than disappear. Many of these jobs can be performed by relatively unskilled workers, whether in rural areas or urban centers. Stream clearance, reforestation, and park main-tenance are some of the traditional work-relief jobs. Many new jobs can be added, such as school aides, health aides, simple main-tenance jobs in public buildings, and renovation of slum areas. These jobs should be in addition to countercyclical job-creation programs designed to help the victims of economic recession. Creating these jobs is costly, however, and the experience of the 1970s suggests that there are limits to saddling public services with inexperienced and unskilled help. There is a continued need to help train the unskilled and to purchase the supportive services associated with training the poor.

Family Planning

While it is tempting to measure antipoverty efforts solely in terms of direct expenditures, the case for a federal role in family planning is a reminder that cost and effectiveness are not always synony-mous. Particularly among the working poor, the size of households rather than the level of family income can be viewed as the key factor in forcing households below the poverty threshold, and programs to help the poor control the size of their families can bring major results in minimizing this trend. If a primary emphasis were placed on family planning efforts that helped the poor fulfill their own desires in reducing the number of unwanted children, at a negligible cost to the public, the next generation would have a far better chance of escaping the grasp of poverty.

Equal Access to Opportunity

While the changes generated by the expansion of the welfare system were only mildly successful in generating institutional change, the elimination of structural barriers to the advancement of the poor must remain a major component of any antipoverty strategy. The vestiges of discrimination continue to block the effective participation of minorities in the American economic system, and they further inhibit the self-advancement of families living in poverty. An effective campaign to reduce—and, it is hoped, obliterate—discrimination in the marketplace would not only bolster the effectiveness of other federal efforts in housing, education, and employment but also free the self-initiated energies of the vast majority of the poor who are genuinely interested in lifting themselves out of poverty. The Civil Rights Act of 1964, the Voting Rights Act of 1965, and related executive orders, if properly enforced, could prove to be more important tools to combat poverty than federal legislation involving massive investments of public funds.

A Floor Beneath Wages

Minimum wage legislation can also play a significant role in reducing poverty. The use of minimum wage provisions must be limited, in that major boosts in minimum wages also tend to reduce overall employment. Nonetheless, there is a persuasive body of evidence showing that the wages of millions of workers tend to cluster around the statutory minimum wage. Prudent increases in the minimum wage, therefore, can assist the working poor and reduce the inherent conflicts between transfer programs and work incentives. Protective legislation cannot be used to transform the nature of the general economy, but it can minimize its worst redistributive effects and have a major impact in promoting equal opportunity in the free market.

A Matter of Priorities

The foregoing agenda for combating poverty omits many needs that traditionally have had claims upon available resources. In some cases, omissions are justified on practical grounds. In other cases, the choices are normative. For example, this list of priorities fails to provide additional expenditures for health care. The omission reflects the judgment that the recent rapid expansion of medicare and medicaid has taxed available health facilities and services. Additional care for poor children is sorely needed, but any major attempt to expand medical services to the poor during the next few years would probably exert added pressures on the costs of existing services and new facilities. The list of priorities also does not include housing improvements for the poor, even though the private housing market is woefully inadequate in providing afford-able housing for low-income families. Further improvements in benefits for the aged are also excluded from the priority agenda, in an attempt to focus on programs that strike at the roots of poverty. This is not to suggest that we can halt our present efforts in these areas, but rather that in a time of scarce resources we must channel additional federal funds in other directions.

Even in the most affluent of societies, difficult and unpleasant choices must be made among a multitude of public needs and goals. Clearly, priorities will have to be set among competing national goals. Although it appeared that the nation had made a commitment in the 1960s to eradicate poverty, support for the drive has not been sustained. In the 1980s, it is difficult to know what additional resources our society will be willing to commit to antipoverty efforts, particularly when the problems of the poor have such a relatively low profile in the American consciousness. Given the serious budgetary constraints and pervasive negativism engendered by the Reagan administration, the assault on poverty certainly is not likely to achieve the preeminence that it enjoyed two decades ago.

During a period of scarce federal resources, many of the poten-tial improvements in the modern welfare system may become possible only through the reallocation of existing programs. The growth of non-means-tested entitlements over the past decade has strained the nation's resources and restricted federal outlays in aid of the poor. As a matter of priorities, it may be necessary in the 1980s to reassess the size and scope of national expenditures for benefits to the non-needy, perhaps reducing payments to upper-income individuals under programs such as social security, medi-care, and unemployment compensation so that the rising tide of poverty in America can be stemmed and eventually reversed. It is important that the middle class does not perceive itself as lacking a stake in the modern welfare system, and yet it is also clear that federal resources must be more carefully husbanded if we are to expand opportunity and alleviate poverty among the least fortunate.

As always, the willingness to commit resources to the problem of poverty is merely a reflection of its relative importance among broader national priorities. Antipoverty efforts have fared poorly in the competition for national resources in recent years. But who can say that our priorities will not change? Who would have predicted in the 1950s that poverty and hunger would be powerful issues in the following two decades, or that the hippies of the 1960s would turn into the yuppies of the 1980s? One can always hope that the noble goal of the Great Society to expand opportunity to all Americans will again rise to the forefront of the national agenda. Only then will the nation meet the challenge voiced by Samuel Johnson over two centuries ago: "A decent provision for the poor is the true test of civilization."

Additional Readings

Bawden, Lee, ed., *The Social Contract Revisited: Aims and Outcomes of President Reagan's Social Welfare Policy*. Washington, D.C.: The Urban Institute, 1984.

Center on Budget and Policy Priorities. *End Results: The Impact of Federal Policies Since 1980 on Low Income Americans*. Washington, D.C.: 1984.

Danziger, Sheldon and Plotnick, Robert. *Has the War on Poverty Been Won?* New York: Academic Press, 1980.

Levitan, Sar A. and Johnson, Clifford M. *Beyond the Safety Net: Reviving the Promise of Opportunity in America*. Cambridge, Mass.: Ballinger/Harper and Row, 1984.

Levitan, Sar A. and Taggart, Robert. *The Promise of Greatness*. Cambridge, Mass.: Harvard University Press, 1976.

Levitan, Sar A. and Wurzburg, Gregory. *Evaluating Federal Social Programs: An Uncertain Art*. Kalamazoo, Mich.: The W. E. Upjohn Institute for Employment Research, 1979.

Murray, Charles. *Losing Ground: American Social Policy 1950–1980*. New York: Basic Books, Inc., 1984.

Palmer, John L. and Sawhill, Isabel V., eds. *The Reagan Record*. Washington, D.C.: The Urban Institute, 1984.

Weicher, John C., ed. *Maintaining the Safety Net: Income Redistribution Programs in the Reagan Administration*. Washington, D.C.: American Enterprise Institute for Public Policy Research, 1984.

Discussion Questions

1. How would you evaluate the legacy of the Great Society?
2. "We stand at the edge of the greatest era in the life of any nation. For the

first time in world history, we have the abundance and the ability to free every man from hopeless want, and to free every person to find fulfillment in the works of his mind or the labor of his hands.

This nation, this people, this generation, has man's first chance to create a Great Society: a society of success without squalor, beauty without barrenness, works of genius without the wretchedness of poverty."

Lyndon B. Johnson, June 26, 1964.

What do you think prevented the realization of President Johnson's vision?
3. What would be your prescription for alleviating poverty in the United States? What would be your order of priorities?
4. "The welfare state is driving the nation to the poorhouse." Evaluate this charge in light of the experience over the past three decades.
5. You are informed that there will be no additional funds for employment and welfare programs during the coming year. If more funds are needed for specific programs, they will have to come from "savings" in other ongoing welfare efforts.
   a. What programs would you cut, if any?
   b. What programs would you expand with the funds saved from the retrenchments?
   c. Would you transfer "savings" to nonwelfare programs or reduce the federal budget deficit?

(No rhetoric, please, about cutting defense. Any cuts must be made from welfare and employment programs. That's a non-negotiable condition for the purpose of this exercise.)

Index

About the Author

Sar A. Levitan is research professor of economics and director of the Center for Social Policy Studies at the George Washington University. He has written more than thirty books, including sixteen published by Johns Hopkins. Among these are *Productivity: Problems, Prospects, and Policies* (with Diane Werneke); *Business Lobbies: The Public Good and the Bottom Line* (with Martha Cooper); and *Working for the Sovereign: Employee Relations in the Federal Government* (with Alexandra B. Noden).

The Johns Hopkins University Press

Programs in Aid of the Poor

This book was composed in Melior by Brushwood Graphics Studio from a design by Martha Farlow. It was printed on 50-lb. Cream White Sebago paper and bound by R. R. Donnelley & Sons Company.